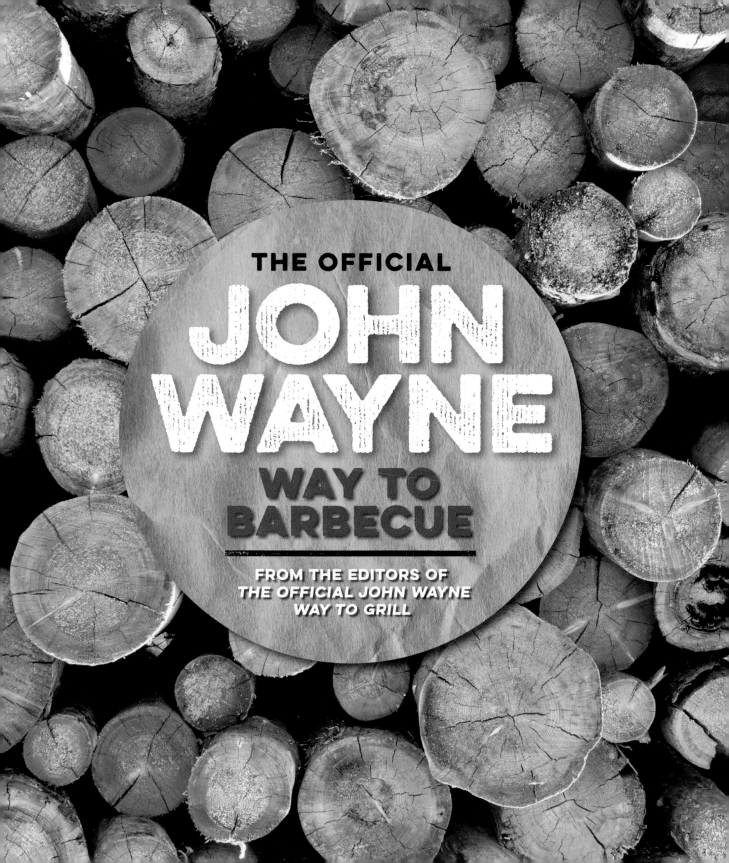

THE OFFICIAL
JOHN WAYNE
WAY TO
BARBECUE

FROM THE EDITORS OF
*THE OFFICIAL JOHN WAYNE
WAY TO GRILL*

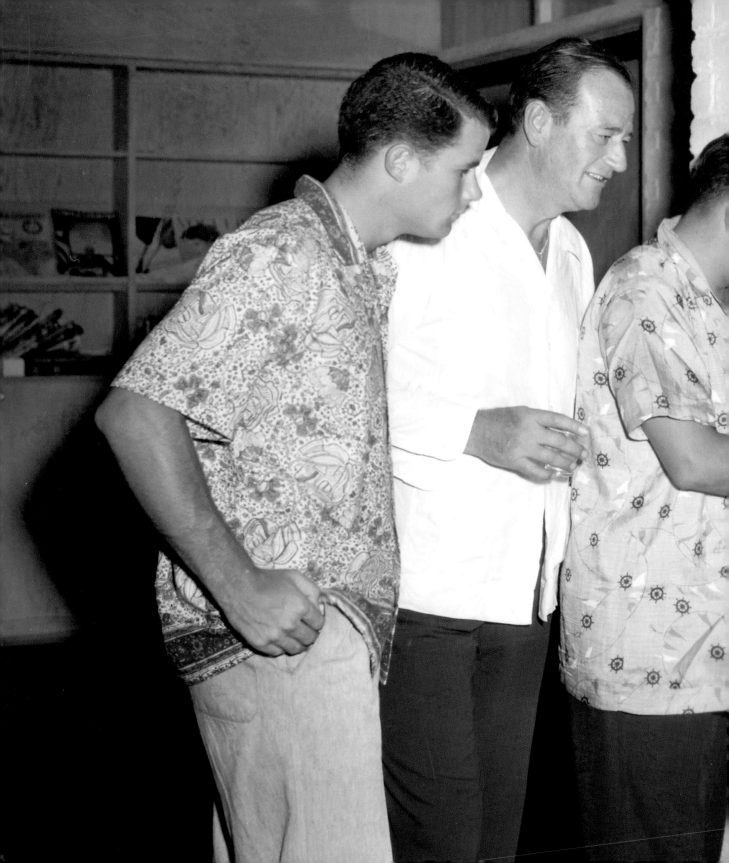

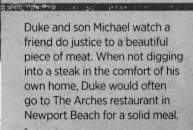

Duke and son Michael watch a friend do justice to a beautiful piece of meat. When not digging into a steak in the comfort of his own home, Duke would often go to The Arches restaurant in Newport Beach for a solid meal.

★

MY FATHER enjoyed tremendous success as a Hollywood icon, but he never lost his appreciation for life's simple, everyday pleasures. Whether it was a weekend spent fishing, a night out with the boys on the town or an afternoon spent at home watching the game on T.V., John Wayne enjoyed a straightforward, no-frills kind of fun. Maybe most of all, my father cherished the taste of good old-fashioned barbecue. He approached cooking like he did everything else in life—with a hearty appetite and a desire to get it right. The following pages contain the recipes, tips and techniques you need to turn your next backyard cookout into a feast Duke would be proud of. Read on and dig in.

Ethan Wayne

Ethan Wayne

John Wayne with youngest son Ethan on the set of the movie *El Dorado* (1966).

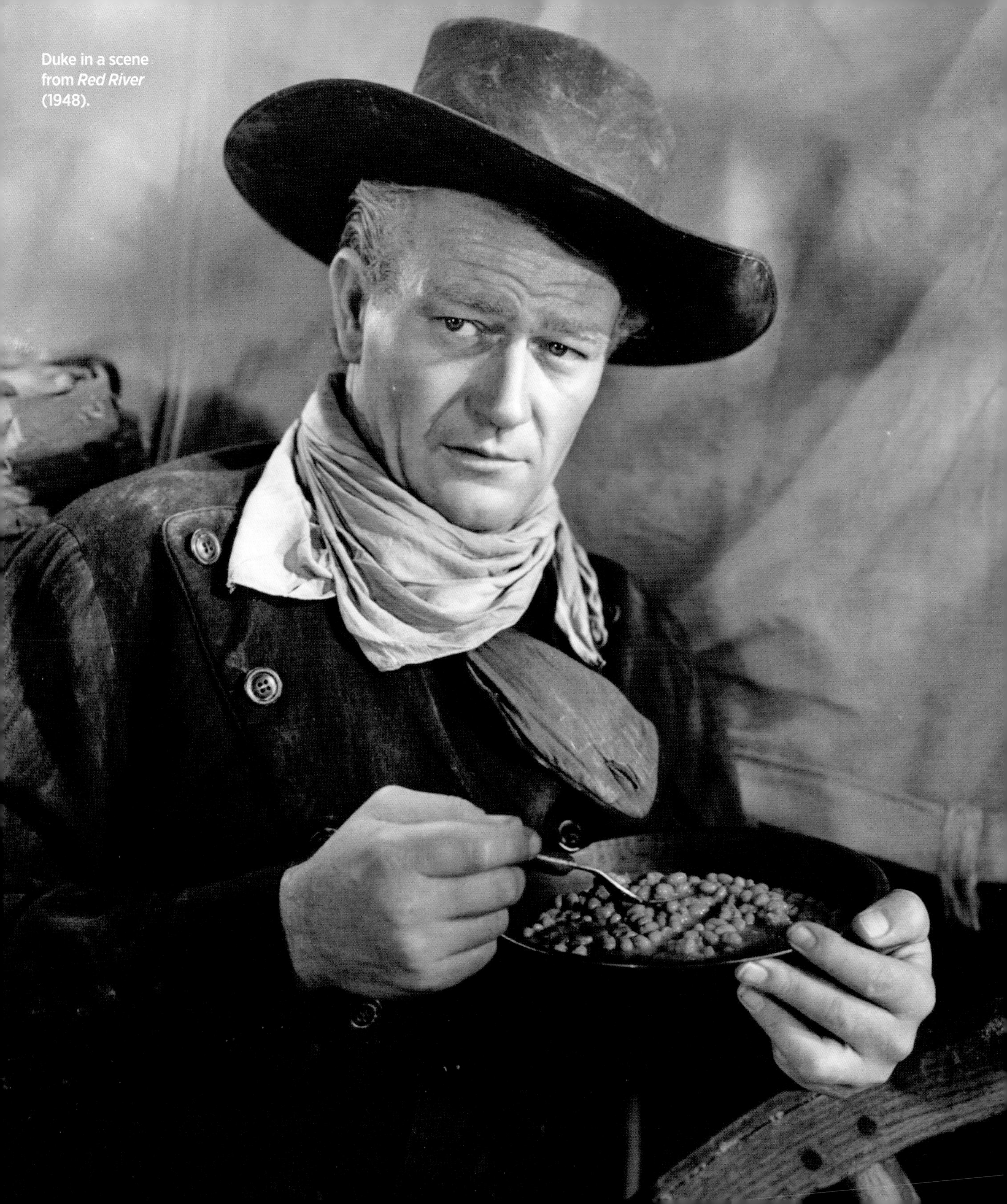

Duke in a scene from *Red River* (1948).

TABLE OF CONTENTS

Hot 'n' Spicy Skirt Steak, Page 60

Conqueror's Chicken Wings pg. 139

Hot 'n' Spicy
Skirt Steak,
Page 60

BEEF

★

DUKE WOULD TIP HIS HAT TO THESE DISHES.

The Man Who Shot Liberty Valance, 1962

DID YOU KNOW?

While it is now considered his signature term of endearment, John Wayne did not utter the nickname "pilgrim" on the silver screen until the 1962 film *The Man Who Shot Liberty Valance*.

GUNSLINGER STEAK SALAD

Add some beefy sizzle to this medley of veggies—it's what Duke would do.

SERVES 6

PROVISIONS

- ½ cup plus 1 Tbsp. barbecue sauce, divided
- 5 Tbsp. olive oil plus more for brushing the vegetables, use divided
- 2 Tbsp. balsamic vinegar, use divided
- 2 lb. flank steak (approximately ¾-in. thick)
- Vegetable oil, for grill
- 2 romaine lettuce hearts
- 1 large radicchio
- 1 large red onion
- Kosher or fine sea salt, to taste
- Pepper, to taste
- 1 pint cherry or pear tomatoes

DIRECTIONS

1. Combine ½ cup barbecue sauce, 2 Tbsp. olive oil and 1 Tbsp. balsamic vinegar and pour into a large plastic food storage bag. Add the flank steak, close the bag and flip several times to coat. Let marinate at room temperature for 20 to 30 minutes or in the refrigerator for up to 12 hours. (If marinating in the refrigerator, let sit at room temperature for 20 to 30 minutes before grilling.)

2. Prepare the grill for direct heat and preheat to medium-high. Brush the grates of the grill with oil. Remove the steak from the marinade and dry with paper towels. Discard the marinade. Grill the steak with the lid of the grill closed for 4 to 5 minutes per side for medium rare. Remove the steak from the grill, place on a platter and cover with foil. Let rest for 15 minutes.

3. While the steak is resting, prepare the salad. Cut the romaine hearts and radicchio into quarters, lengthwise. Slice the onion into ½-inch-thick slices. Brush with some olive oil and sprinkle with a little salt and pepper. Place the onions on the grill and cook with the lid closed for 5 minutes. Turn the onion slices over, add the lettuce and radicchio and cook for about 5 minutes (along with the onions) turning 3 or 4 times or until slightly wilted with some brown spots. Remove from grill and cut the lettuce into large chunks. Separate the onion rings. Whisk together the 3 Tbsp. olive oil, 1 Tbsp. balsamic vinegar and 1 Tbsp. barbecue sauce together in a large mixing bowl. Add the lettuce, radicchio and onions and toss to coat. Place on a platter. Slice the steak thinly across the grain and place on top of the salad. Scatter tomatoes around.

ALL-AMERICAN BEEF TENDERLOIN

Nothing embodies our country's plentiful bounty like a thick, juicy slab of beef.

SERVES 8 TO 10

PROVISIONS

HORSERADISH SAUCE

- ¾ cup sour cream
- ¼ cup prepared horseradish
- 2 Tbsp. fresh lemon juice
- ½ tsp. pepper
- ¼ tsp. kosher or fine sea salt

TENDERLOIN

- 1 whole beef tenderloin, trimmed, about 5 lb.
- 4 Tbsp. olive oil
- 6 cloves garlic, minced
- 3 Tbsp. minced thyme
- 3 Tbsp. minced rosemary
- 2 tsp. kosher or fine sea salt
- 1 tsp. pepper
- Vegetable oil, for grill

DIRECTIONS

1. Combine the sour cream, horseradish, lemon juice, ½ tsp. pepper and ¼ tsp. salt. Mix well and refrigerate covered until ready to serve.

2. Remove the tenderloin from the refrigerator an hour before planning to grill. Trim any excess fat with a sharp knife. Tuck the thin end under to approximate the thickness of the rest of the tenderloin. Tie with butcher's twine every couple of inches to help the roast keep its shape.

3. Combine the olive oil, garlic, herbs, salt and pepper. Spread the mixture all over the tenderloin, including the ends, wrap in plastic wrap and let sit at room temperature for about an hour.

4. Prepare the grill for direct heat and preheat to medium-high. Brush the grates with vegetable oil. Remove the tenderloin from the plastic wrap and place on the grill, close the lid and cook for 6 to 8 minutes on all four sides, approximately 30 minutes in total. During the last phase of cooking, start checking the temperature of the meat by inserting an instant-read thermometer into the center. Take the meat off the grill when it reaches 125 degrees F for medium rare. Cover with foil and let rest for 10 to 15 minutes before removing the twine and slicing.

5. Slice the beef and serve with horseradish sauce.

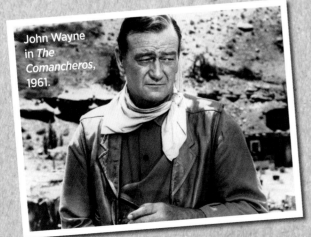

John Wayne in *The Comancheros*, 1961.

WAYNE FAMILY TIP

Using a meat thermometer when grilling meat is always a good idea but is particularly important when grilling an expensive cut of meat such as tenderloin, as overcooking can ruin it.

RINGO KID'S SKIRT STEAK

Take your tastebuds on a wild ride with this hearty dish.

SERVES 6

PROVISIONS

- 4 Tbsp. brown sugar
- 2 Tbsp. kosher salt
- 2 Tbsp. smoked paprika
- 1 Tbsp. garlic powder
- 2 tsp. cayenne pepper
- 2½ lb. skirt steak
- Vegetable oil, for grill

DIRECTIONS

1. In a small mixing bowl, combine the brown sugar, salt, paprika, garlic powder and cayenne pepper. Press the mixture generously on both sides of the skirt steak. Let sit at room temperature while preparing the grill.

2. Prepare grill for direct heat. Brush the grill grates with oil.

3. Pat the steak dry and grill for 2 to 3 minutes per side for medium rare. Cover the steak with foil and let rest for 10 minutes before slicing.

Duke and Claire Trevor in *Stagecoach* (1939).

DID YOU KNOW?

Duke's popularity remains unmatched more than 35 years after his death. He is the only deceased actor to consistently place in the Harris Poll's list of top 10 favorite actors.

ROOSTER'S SHORT RIB BURGERS

Even the most hard-nosed, no-nonsense barbecue fans
will be lining up for a second serving of these ground rounds.

SERVES 6

PROVISIONS

CARAMELIZED ONIONS

- 2½ lb. white or yellow onions (3 large)
- 2 Tbsp. unsalted butter
- 2 Tbsp. olive oil
- ½ tsp. kosher or fine sea salt
- ¼ tsp. pepper
- 4 sprigs fresh thyme
- 2 Tbsp. balsamic vinegar

SPICY MAYONNAISE

- ¾ cup mayonnaise
- 2 Tbsp. Sriracha sauce

BURGERS

- 1 lb. ground boneless beef short ribs
- 1 lb. ground skirt steak or tri-trip
- Vegetable oil, for patties
- Kosher or fine sea salt, to taste
- Pepper, to taste
- 6 Kaiser rolls
- 3 Tbsp. melted butter
- 6 lettuce leaves
- 6 slices tomato

DIRECTIONS

CARAMELIZED ONIONS

1. Cut onions in half and thinly slice. Heat butter and oil together in a large skillet over medium-low. Add the sliced onions, salt, pepper and thyme. Cook the onions slowly, stirring occasionally, until deeply browned and caramelized, about 45 minutes. Remove the thyme sprigs, raise heat to high and add the balsamic vinegar. Cook, stirring, until all the vinegar has evaporated. Can be made several days ahead and stored in a covered container in the refrigerator. Reheat in microwave or on stove-top before using.

SPICY MAYONNAISE

1. Mix the mayonnaise and Sriracha together until fully combined. Refrigerate until ready to serve.

BURGERS

1. Prepare grill for direct heat. Combine the ground meats. Divide into 6 equal portions and shape into patties about ¾-in. thick. Make a deep depression in the center of the patties. Brush both sides of the patties with oil and season with salt and pepper. Grill for 4 minutes, flip the burgers and grill for another 4 to 5 minutes for medium rare.

2. Cut the Kaiser rolls in half, spread the cut surfaces with melted butter and grill for 1 to 2 minutes.

3. To serve, spread the bottom roll with some of the mayonnaise mixture, top with lettuce, tomato slice, burger patty and some caramelized onions.

DID YOU KNOW?

Out of all the roles in Duke's career, Rooster Cogburn was the only one he played twice—first in *True Grit* (1969) and again in its sequel *Rooster Cogburn* (1975).

BRANNIGAN'S LONDON BROIL

Detective Brannigan was relentless in his pursuit of justice.
This London broil is relentless in its pursuit of leaving you full and satisfied.

SERVES 6

PROVISIONS

1 (2- to 2½-lb.) London broil

Vegetable oil, for grill

BLUE CHEESE SAUCE

⅔ cup sour cream

⅓ cup mayonnaise

2 tsp. Worcestershire sauce

4 oz. crumbled blue cheese

Kosher or fine sea salt and pepper, to taste

MARINADE

½ cup olive oil

¼ cup soy sauce

¼ cup red wine vinegar

1 Tbsp. Dijon mustard

1 Tbsp. Worcestershire sauce

2 garlic cloves, minced

DIRECTIONS

BLUE CHEESE SAUCE

1. Combine all ingredients in a mixing bowl. Season to taste with salt and pepper. Cover with plastic wrap and refrigerate until ready to serve.

MARINADE

1. Whisk all ingredients together in a mixing bowl. Pour the marinade into a plastic food storage bag. Place the London broil in the bag, flipping several times to coat the meat with the marinade.

Let sit at room temperature for 30 minutes or refrigerate for up to 24 hours. If marinating in the refrigerator, let sit at room temperature for 20 to 30 minutes before grilling.

STEAK

1. Prepare the grill for direct heat and preheat to medium-high.

2. Remove the meat from the marinade, discarding the marinade and pat dry with paper towels.

3. Brush the grates of the grill with oil and grill the meat 6 to 8 minutes per side, with the lid open, or until it reaches an internal temperature of 125 degrees F for medium-rare. Place the meat on a cutting board, cover with foil and let rest for 10 minutes before serving. Slice thinly across the grain and serve with the blue cheese sauce.

DID YOU KNOW?

While many of his characters fearlessly wielded firearms to fend off wrongdoers, John Wayne only portrayed a police officer in two films, 1974's *McQ* and 1975's *Brannigan*.

RED RIVER RIB EYE

You don't have to survive a long, treacherous cattle drive to deserve this juicy cut.

SERVES 4

PROVISIONS

Vegetable oil, for grill

4 (10-oz.) boneless rib eye steaks, 1-in. thick

COFFEE RUB

2 Tbsp. finely ground coffee

2 Tbsp. chili powder

1 Tbsp. light or dark brown sugar

1½ tsp. pepper

1 tsp. kosher or fine sea salt

1 lb. ground chuck (80 percent lean)

1 lb. ground brisket

Kosher or fine sea salt, to taste

DIRECTIONS

1. Combine all the rub ingredients together in a small bowl.

2. Remove steaks from the refrigerator, brush all sides with oil. Rub and press the rub into all sides of the steaks. Let sit at room temperature for 20 to 30 minutes.

3. Prepare grill for direct heat and preheat to high. Brush the grates with oil.

4. Grill steaks 4 to 6 minutes per side or until they reach an internal temperature of 125 degrees F for medium rare.

5. Let steaks rest for 5 to 10 minutes before serving.

DID YOU KNOW?

John Wayne couldn't afford steak as a child as his family often struggled to make ends meet. But once Duke pulled himself up by the bootstraps, he made sure he and his could enjoy steak as often as they wanted.

John Wayne as cattle rancher Thomas Dunson in the 1948 film, *Red River*.

John Wayne takes a break from riding the range on his ranch with some pals. The 26 Bar Ranch, which the actor purchased in the mid 1960s, spanned 50,000 acres and was home to 80,000 head of cattle.

WAYNE FAMILY TIP

For the sake of both flavor and simplicity, do all of your prep work the day before you grill. Meat tastes best when it's left in its marinade overnight and put on the grill at room temperature.

SIZZLIN' STEAK SKEWERS

The best part about eating your steak on a skewer?
It frees up a hand to hold a cold beverage, just like Duke would want.

MAKES 24 TO 26 SKEWERS

PROVISIONS

24–26 wooden skewers

2 lb. skirt steak

MARINADE

⅓ cup olive oil

2 Tbsp. lime juice

1 tsp. ground cumin

½ tsp. kosher or fine sea salt

¼ tsp. pepper

PESTO

2 garlic cloves, roughly chopped

1 jalapeño pepper, seeded, deveined and chopped

¼ cup pine nuts

4 cups fresh cilantro

4 Tbsp. lime juice (from 2 limes)

1 Tbsp agave or honey

1 tsp. kosher or fine sea salt

½ tsp. pepper

6 Tbsp. olive oil

Vegetable oil, for grill

DIRECTIONS

1. Soak the skewers in water for 30 to 45 minutes.

2. Cut the steak into 8-in. lengths. Lay on a plate or baking sheet in a single layer and place in the freezer for 30 to 45 minutes to make slicing easier. Remove from freezer and slice lengthwise into ¼-in. pieces. Let sit at room temperature while making the marinade.

MARINADE

1. Whisk all the marinade ingredients together in a small mixing bowl. Pour into a large freezer bag, add the sliced steak and toss a few times to coat. Let rest at room temperature for 20 to 30 minutes.

PESTO

1. Place the garlic, jalapeño, and pine nuts in a food processor. Process until everything is finely ground. Add the cilantro, lime juice, agave, salt and pepper. Process until fully combined.

Add the olive oil and process until nearly smooth. Place in a serving bowl.

STEAK

1. Prepare the grill for direct heat and preheat to high.

2. Remove the steak from the marinade. Discard the marinade and thread the steak onto the pre-soaked skewers.

3. Brush grill grates with oil. Grill the skewers 1 to 2 minutes per side keeping the lid to the grill open. Serve with the pesto.

John Wayne in
The Cowboys, 1972.

TEXAS TACOS

These tasty morsels are just like the Lone Star state—big and full of flavor.

MAKES 12 TACOS

PROVISIONS

SALSA

- 2 jalapeños
- 6 plum tomatoes, cut in half lengthwise
- 1 small red onion, sliced ¼-inch thick
- 4 Tbsp. lime juice
- ½ tsp. kosher or fine sea salt
- ½ cup cilantro leaves
-    Vegetable oil, for tomatoes

TACOS

- 12 corn tortillas
-     Vegetable oil, for grill
- 1½ lb. flank or skirt steak
-     Kosher or fine sea salt, to taste
-     Pepper, to taste
- ½   small red or white onion, finely diced
- ½   cup cilantro leaves, finely chopped

DIRECTIONS

SALSA

1. Prepare grill for direct heat and preheat to high.

2. Place the jalapeños directly on the grill. Cook with lid down, turning occasionally, until the skin is charred all over, about 10 to 12 minutes. Take off the grill, place in a small bowl and cover with plastic wrap. Let rest at least 5 minutes.

3. Brush the cut sides of the tomatoes with oil and place directly on the grill. Brush both sides of the onion with oil and place directly on the grill. Grill with the lid closed until the tomatoes are a little charred and starting to soften, about 10 minutes. Grill the onions, flipping once, until charred and beginning to soften. Keep the grill lit.

4. Rub the jalapeños to remove the charred skin. For a mild salsa, cut in half and scrap out the seeds. Place in a blender or food processor with the grilled tomatoes and onions. Add the lime juice and blend until smooth, scraping down the sides of container as needed. Add the cilantro and pulse several times, you want to still see flecks of the cilantro. Place in a serving bowl.

TACOS

1. Wrap the tortillas in foil and place on the top rack of the grill or on the coolest side to warm them.

2. Brush the grill grates with oil.

3. Season the steak with salt and pepper and grill with the lid open for 2 minutes per side. Let sit 5 minutes before serving. Cut the steak into thin slices.

4. Serve the meat in the tortillas with the onion and cilantro and the salsa on the side.

John Wayne in the 1960 film *The Alamo*, which he also directed.

NO-FUSS FILET MIGNON

Enjoy the taste of one of the most delicious cuts of meat around without any bit of hassle.

SERVES 4

PROVISIONS

CHIVE BUTTER

- 6 Tbsp. butter, at room temperature
- 2 Tbsp. minced chives

STEAK

- 4 filet mignon steaks, 1½-in. thick, about 6 oz. each
- Olive oil, for steak
- Kosher or fine sea salt, to taste
- Pepper, to taste
- Vegetable oil, for grill

DIRECTIONS

CHIVE BUTTER

1. In a small mixing bowl, mash the butter with a fork. Add the chives and mix well. Place a piece of plastic wrap on a flat work surface, and scoop the butter on to the plastic wrap. Roll into a cylinder and twist the ends of plastic wrap. Refrigerate at least 30 minutes. Can be made a week in advance and stored in the refrigerator.

STEAK

1. Remove the steaks from the refrigerator half an hour before you plan to grill them. Drizzle with olive oil on all sides and season generously with salt and pepper. Let sit at room temperature for about 30 minutes.

2. Prepare grill for direct heat and preheat to medium-high. Brush the grates with oil. Grill the steaks with the lid closed for 3 to 5 minutes per side (internal temperature of between 125–130 degrees F) for medium rare.

3. Let steaks rest for 5 minutes. Cut the butter into 4 slices and place one slice on each steak. Serve immediately.

Duke in *Flame of Barbary Coast*, 1945.

WAYNE FAMILY TIP

Most of your seasoning will be lost to the grill grates when you cook steaks, so don't be afraid to season your meat with gusto.

FREEDOM FAJITAS

Any flag-waving patriot knows American cuisine is made great by influences from around the globe, and these fajitas are evidence of that.

SERVES 6

PROVISIONS

MARINADE

- ¾ cup olive oil
- ½ cup orange juice
- ¼ cup lime juice
- 1 jalapeño, minced
- 2 garlic cloves, minced
- 1 tsp. ground cumin
- 1 tsp. dried oregano
- 1 tsp. kosher or fine sea salt
- ½ tsp. pepper

FAJITAS

- 2 lb. skirt steak
- 1 large onion, thinly sliced
- 1 green bell pepper, seeded, deveined and thinly sliced
- 1 red bell pepper, seeded, deveined and thinly sliced
- 1 yellow or orange bell pepper, seeded, deveined and thinly sliced
- 1 Tbsp. vegetable oil, plus more to prepare grill
- Salt and pepper, to taste
- 12 flour tortillas or 24 corn tortillas, warmed

FOR SERVING, OPTIONAL

- Salsa
- Sour cream
- Avocado slices
- Guacamole
- Grated cheese

DIRECTIONS

1. Combine all the marinade ingredients in a mixing bowl and whisk well.

2. Place the steak in a large food storage bag, pour in half the marinade and seal.

3. Place the onions and peppers in another large food storage bag, pour in the rest of the marinade and seal. Place the steak and vegetables in the refrigerator, laying the bags flat and marinate for 4 hours, flipping the bags occasionally.

4. Prepare the grill for direct heat and preheat to medium-high.

5. Drain and discard the marinade from the steak and vegetables. Brush the grates with oil and cook the steak 2 to 3 minutes per side with the lid closed. Remove from grill, place on a cutting board, cover with foil and let sit for 10 minutes.

6. While the steak is resting, prepare the vegetables. Place a cast-iron skillet directly on the grill and let it heat. Add 1 Tbsp. of vegetable oil and let that get hot. Add the vegetables and cook, stirring occasionally, until softened, about 7 minutes. Alternately, you can cook the vegetables on the stove.

7. Slice the steak thinly and serve with the vegetables and warmed tortillas.

John Wayne in a scene from *The Lucky Texan*, 1934.

DID YOU KNOW?

Nearly 2,500 horses were used in filming *The Undefeated* (1969). John Wayne sustained a shoulder injury when he fell off one of his equine costars.

BLT STEAK SANDWICH

The classic sandwich goes from good to great once you add Duke's favorite ingredient: steak.

SERVES 6

PROVISIONS

BACON MAYONNAISE

- 1 cup mayonnaise
- 6 slices bacon, cooked, crumbled and cooled
- 2 Tbsp. minced chives
- 1 tsp. red wine vinegar
  Salt and pepper, to taste

STEAK

- ½ cup olive oil
- ¼ cup red wine vinegar
- 2 Tbsp. Worcestershire sauce
- ½ tsp. kosher or fine sea salt
- ½ tsp. pepper
- 1½ lb. flank steaks
  Vegetable oil, for grill

SANDWICHES

- 6 hoagie rolls
- 2 tomatoes, sliced
- 1 cup baby arugula

DIRECTIONS

BACON MAYONNAISE

1. Combine the mayonnaise, bacon, chives and red wine vinegar. Season to taste with salt and pepper. Refrigerate covered until ready to serve.

STEAK

1. Combine olive oil with vinegar, Worcestershire sauce, salt and pepper. Pour into a large food storage bag, add the flank steak and flip several times to coat. Let marinate at room temperature for 20 to 30 minutes or in the refrigerator for up to 12 hours. (If marinating in the refrigerator, let sit at room temperature for 20 to 30 minutes before grilling.)

2. Prepare the grill for direct heat and preheat to medium-high. Brush the grates of the grill with oil. Remove the steak from the marinade and dry with paper towels. Discard the marinade. Grill the steak with the lid closed for 4 to 5 minutes per side for medium rare. Remove the steak from the grill, place on a platter and cover with foil. Let rest for 15 minutes. Slice the hoagie rolls and lightly grill the cut sides for 10 to 20 seconds.

3. Thinly slice the steak across the grain.

4. Spread both sides of the hoagie rolls with the bacon mayonnaise. Top with steak, tomato slices and arugula.

Duke in *The Undefeated*, 1969.

BEEF JERKY

Worthy of the truest cowboy, this jerky is something you'll want to have in your satchel when you need a simple, satisfying snack.

MAKES ABOUT 2 LB. OF JERKY

PROVISIONS

- 2 lb. boneless sirloin, about 1-in. thick
- 1 (15-oz.) can dark cherries in syrup
- 1 cup cola (not diet)
- ⅓ cup honey
- ¼ cup soy sauce
- ¼ cup balsamic vinegar
- 2 tsp. chipotle pepper powder
- 1 Tbsp. kosher or fine sea
- 1 tsp. black pepper

DIRECTIONS

1. Place the sirloin in the freezer for about 45 minutes to make it easier to slice.

2. Puree the cherries with their liquid in a blender until smooth. In a heavy saucepan, combine the pureed cherries with the cola, honey, soy sauce, vinegar, chipotle pepper powder, salt and pepper. Bring to a simmer over medium heat. Let simmer for 20 minutes or until reduced to about 2 cups. Let cool.

3. Cut the meat into strips about ½-in. wide. Place the cut meat in a large food storage bag, pour in the cooled marinade and refrigerate overnight or up to 3 days. Remove meat from marinade, pat the meat dry and discard the marinade.

4. Prepare smoker for low heat (between 175–200 degrees F).

5. Lay the meat strips on the grill in a single layer, making sure they do not overlap. Smoke for 6 to 8 hours or until the edges appear dry and there is a hint of moisture in the center of the slices.

6. Store in an airtight container for up to 2 weeks in the refrigerator.

WAYNE FAMILY TIP

If you don't have a smoker, you can still achieve the same effect with your charcoal or gas grill. For charcoal grills, use half as much charcoal as you usually would and place smoked wood chips next to (not on) the coals. Cover the grill with its lid and adjust the top and bottom vents to regulate the heat while you cook the meat. Gas grill owners should place smoked wood chips on an aluminum pan (or inside tinfoil patches) and place in a cooler section of the grill while you cook the meat on a higher-temperature section.

Duke in *Rio Bravo*, 1950.

Lee Marvin, Jimmy Stewart and Duke in a scene from *The Man Who Shot Liberty Valance* (1962). Duke's Tom Doniphon shows his mettle by insisting outlaw Valance (Marvin) pick up a dropped steak. Marvin and Duke would work together again in *Donovan's Reef* the next year.

GRILLED MEATLOAF

Go for this hearty meal when you need a break from burgers and steaks.

SERVES 6 TO 8

PROVISIONS

- 2 cups panko breadcrumbs
- 1 cup milk
- 1½ lb. ground chuck
- 1½ lb. ground pork
- 1 medium onion
- 2 large eggs
- 2 tsp. salt
- 1 tsp. dried oregano
- 1 tsp. garlic powder
- 1 tsp. pepper
- ¼ cup ketchup
- ¼ cup barbecue sauce

DIRECTIONS

1. Prepare grill for indirect heat and preheat to medium (350–400 degrees F).

2. Place the breadcrumbs in a large mixing bowl. Add the milk and stir. Add the beef and pork. Using the large holes of a box grater, grate the onion into the bowl. Add the eggs, salt, oregano, garlic powder and pepper. Mix well.

3. Combine the ketchup and barbecue sauce in a small bowl and set aside.

4. Stack two 2-foot-long pieces of heavy duty foil on top of each other. Spray the top sheet with nonstick cooking spray. Place the meatloaf mixture in the center of the foil and shape into a loaf about 10 by 6 inches. Fold the foil tightly around the meatloaf, sealing all the edges.

5. Place on the grill and cook with the lid closed for about 1 hour, maintaining a temperature of between 350 and 400 degrees F. After an hour, unwrap the foil and check the internal temperature of the meatloaf. If it is 160 degrees F, remove the foil and, using a long sturdy spatula, place the meatloaf directly on the grill (if not 160 degrees F, re-wrap and continue cooking), brush with the ketchup barbecue sauce mixture, close the lid and cook for another 10 minutes.

6. Let the meatloaf sit for 5 minutes before serving.

GAUCHO STEAK

Once John Wayne could afford steak, he made it an essential part of his diet.
Once your family tries this sizzling variation, they'll never want to go without it either.

SERVES 4

PROVISIONS

CHIMICHURRI

- 2 cups packed flat leaf parsley
- 2 garlic cloves, chopped
- 1 tsp. dried oregano
- 1 tsp. kosher or fine sea salt, plus more to taste
- ½ tsp. pepper, plus more to taste
- ½ tsp. crushed red pepper flakes
- 4 Tbsp. lemon juice (2 lemons)
- 2 Tbsp. sherry vinegar
- ⅔ cup olive oil

STEAK

- 2 lb. skirt steak
- Vegetable oil, for grill

DIRECTIONS

1. Combine the parsley, garlic, oregano, salt, pepper, red pepper flakes, lemon juice and vinegar in a blender or food processor; process until almost smooth. Add the olive oil and blend. Taste and add more salt and pepper if desired. Take ½ cup of the chimichurri to marinate the steak and reserve the rest for serving.

2. Coat the steak with ½ cup chimichurri, rubbing it into the meat. Cover with plastic wrap and let sit at room temperature for 20 to 30 minutes.

3. Prepare grill for direct heat and preheat to medium-high. Brush the grates with oil. Place the steak on the grill (do not remove the marinade) and grill 2 to 3 minutes per side with the lid closed. Let sit for 5 to 10 minutes before slicing.

4. Slice the steak and serve with the reserved chimichurri sauce.

John Wayne in *Hondo* (1953).

DOWNHOME RIBS

Great ribs are the mark of a true pit master, and these will help you become the "genuine article."

SERVES 6

PROVISIONS

RIBS

- 1 white onion, chopped
- 4 garlic cloves, smashed
- 2 bay leaves
- 5–6 lb. beef back ribs
- Kosher or fine sea salt, to taste
- Pepper, to taste

BARBECUE SAUCE

- ½ cup spicy brown mustard
- ½ cup apple cider vinegar
- ⅓ cup brown sugar, packed
- 6 Tbsp. ketchup
- 3 Tbsp. melted butter
- 3 Tbsp. Worcestershire sauce
- 1 Tbsp. garlic powder

DIRECTIONS

1. Fill a large pot with water, add the onion, garlic and bay leaves. Bring to a boil. Cut the ribs so they fit in the pot. Add to the boiling water, reduce heat, cover and simmer for 45 to 60 minutes or until fork tender.

2. While the ribs are boiling, prepare the barbecue sauce. Combine all the sauce ingredients in a saucepan and whisk to combine. Heat over medium until warm, about 4 minutes.

3. Prepare the grill for direct heat and preheat to high.

4. Remove the ribs from the cooking water and pat dry. Season the ribs with salt and pepper and place on a baking sheet. Brush with barbecue sauce.

5. Place the ribs on the grill and cook 2 minutes per side (for a total of 8 minutes) basting with more sauce each time you flip them.

John Wayne in *El Dorado* (1966).

DID YOU KNOW?

El Dorado was the third of five films on which director Howard Hawks teamed up with John Wayne. Their first outing, *Red River*, was in 1948 and their last was *Rio Lobo* in 1970.

RIO BRAVO BEEF KEBOBS

You may already be an authority on beef, but these kebobs will earn you a sheriff's badge.

SERVES 6

PROVISIONS

TARRAGON AIOLI

- ¾ cup mayonnaise
- 2 Tbsp. red wine vinegar
- 2 garlic cloves, minced
- 3 Tbsp. finely chopped fresh tarragon
- ½ tsp. pepper
  Kosher or fine sea salt, to taste

KEBOBS

- ½ cup olive oil
- ¼ cup red wine vinegar
- 1 tsp. garlic powder
- 1 tsp. onion powder
- ½ tsp. kosher or fine sea salt
- ½ tsp. pepper
- 1½ lb. sirloin, cut into 1 ½-in. pieces
- 1 lb. white button mushrooms
- 1 green bell pepper, cut into 1-in. chunks
- 1 red bell pepper, cut into 1-in. chunks
- 1 small red onion, cut into wedges

DIRECTIONS

TARRAGON AIOLI

1. Combine all the aioli ingredients in a small bowl. Cover and refrigerate until ready to serve.

KEBOBS

1. Combine olive oil, red wine vinegar, garlic and onion powders, salt and pepper in a large mixing bowl. Add the cut sirloin and mushrooms. Stir to ensure the meat and mushrooms are well coated. Cover bowl with plastic wrap and allow to marinate for 30 minutes at room temperature.

2. Prepare grill for direct heat and preheat to medium-high.

3. Remove meat and mushrooms from bowl and discard the marinade. Thread the meat, mushrooms, peppers and onions onto 6 metal skewers alternating meat and vegetables.

4. Grill with lid closed 2 to 3 minutes on 4 sides for a total of 8 to 12 minutes.

5. Serve the kebobs with the aioli.

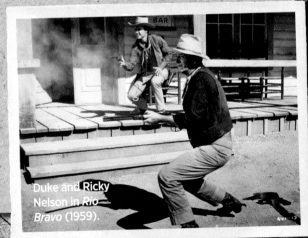

Duke and Ricky Nelson in *Rio Bravo* (1959).

WAYNE FAMILY TIP

If you prefer to use wooden skewers over metal ones, make sure you soak them in water for at least 30 minutes prior to cooking. This will help prevent the skewers from catching fire!

WAR WAGON BURGERS

These ground rounds will help you fuel up before you hit the trails.

SERVES 8

PROVISIONS

- 1 (8-count) pkg. refrigerated ready-to-bake jumbo biscuits
- 2 Tbsp. melted butter
- 1 cup canned chili
- 3 lb. ground chuck (80 percent lean)
  Vegetable oil, for patties
  Kosher or fine sea salt, to taste
  Pepper, to taste
- 1 cup shredded cheddar cheese
- ½ cup chopped onion

DIRECTIONS

1. Bake the biscuits according to the package directions. Cut in half, brush the cut sides with melted butter and keep warm.

2. Prepare the grill for direct heat and heat to medium-high. Place the chili in a saucepan and heat on the grill or on the stove. Keep warm.

3. Divide the meat into 8 equal portions. Form each portion loosely into a ¾-inch-thick patty and make a depression in the center of each patty with your thumb. Brush the patties with oil and season generously with salt and pepper.

4. Grill the burgers 3 to 4 minutes per side for medium rare. Serve the burgers on the biscuits topped with chili, grated cheese and chopped onion.

Kirk Douglas and John Wayne in *The War Wagon* (1967).

DID YOU KNOW?

Kirk Douglas appeared with John Wayne in two films prior to *The War Wagon*, *In Harm's Way* (1965) and *Cast a Giant Shadow* (1966).

BIG JAKE'S BIG BRISKET

You don't need to be a tough-as-nails gunslinger to help yourself to this delicious hunk of meat.

SERVES 8

PROVISIONS

5   lb. brisket with at least ½-in. fat cap

Kosher or fine sea salt, to taste

Pepper, to taste

DIRECTIONS

1. Season the brisket liberally on all sides with salt and pepper. Wrap in plastic wrap and refrigerate 12 to 24 hours. Remove the brisket from refrigerator 30 minutes before smoking.

2. Prepare your smoker with hickory fuel.* Unwrap the brisket, place on the smoker fat side up and smoke between 180–220 degrees F for 6 to 12 hours. The lower the heat, the longer the cooking time, and the more smoke flavor you will have. Smoke the brisket until it reaches an internal temperature between 195 and 205 degrees F.

3. Wrap in foil or butcher paper and let rest 20 minutes before serving.

*If you don't have a smoker, refer to the Wayne Family Tip on page 36 for making this recipe without one.

John Wayne in *Big Jake* (1971).

WAYNE FAMILY TIP

If you feel your briskets are a little on the dry side, you may be trimming too much fat off the meat. Besides adding flavor, fat helps insulate the meat from the fire and prevents those precious juices from escaping.

HOMESTEADER STEAK

This steak dinner doesn't require any fancy frills or fixings. It's simply delicious.

SERVES 2

PROVISIONS

- 1 (2- to 3-lb.) bone-in rib eye steak
- Olive oil, for steak
- Kosher or fine sea salt, to taste
- Pepper, to taste
- ½ cup butter
- 6 garlic cloves, smashed

DIRECTIONS

1. Take the steak out of the refrigerator 45 to 60 minutes before planning to cook. Rub the steak all over with olive oil. Season generously with salt and pepper making sure to season the sides of the steak as well as the top and bottom. Let sit.

2. Prepare the grill for direct heat and preheat to high. Preheat oven to 375 degrees F.

3. In a small saucepan melt the butter with the garlic over low heat.

4. Place the steak on the grill. Grill with the lid open for 3 minutes, then give it a quarter turn. Grill 3 more minutes, then flip over and grill 3 minutes, turn it a quarter turn and grill 3 more minutes for a total of 12 minutes.

5. Place the steak on a baking sheet, brush with the garlic butter and place in the oven. Baste the steak with garlic butter every 5 minutes. After 15 minutes, flip the steak over and continue to cook, basting every 5 minutes.

6. After 20 minutes total in the oven start checking temperature with an instant-read thermometer inserted into the thickest part of the meat. When it reaches 130–135 degrees F, remove from oven, give it another basting with butter, and let rest for 10 minutes before serving.

7. Give the steak a final brush with the garlic butter before serving with chimichurri (see page 42) if desired.

Duke in *The Fighting Kentuckian* (1949).

DID YOU KNOW?

John Wayne spent part of his boyhood on a farm near Lancaster, California. To get to school, he would ride a pony named Jenny into town.

GRILLED STEAK WITH GARLIC AND SPINACH

Sure, John Wayne would eat his veggies,
just as long as they were served alongside a hunk of meat like this steak.

SERVES 4

PROVISIONS

12 garlic cloves, peeled and left whole

½ cup olive oil

4 (8- to 10-oz.) boneless New York strip steaks,
1–1¼ in. thick

Kosher or fine sea salt, to taste

Pepper, to taste

1 lb. spinach leaves

Duke gets ready
to throw down.

DIRECTIONS

1. Combine garlic and olive oil in a small saucepan and cook at a low simmer until garlic starts to brown, about 15 to 20 minutes. Remove from heat and let cool.

2. Remove steaks from refrigerator and let sit at room temperature for 30 minutes. Prepare grill for direct heat and heat to medium-high.

3. Brush the steaks with some of the garlic oil and season them generously with salt and pepper on both sides.

4. Grill the steaks 3 to 4 minutes per side with the lid closed, or until they reach an internal temperature of 125 degrees F for medium rare. Let sit for 10 minutes before serving.

5. While the steaks are resting, place a large cast-iron skillet on the grill over direct heat. Heat 2 Tbsp. of the garlic oil in the pan until it starts to shimmer then add as much of the spinach as will fit in the pan. Cook, tossing, until it starts to wilt, adding more spinach until all of it is in the pan. Cook the spinach just until wilted but still bright green, add in the garlic cloves and season with salt and pepper. Serve the steaks on the spinach.

WAYNE FAMILY TIP

Using lighter fluid to help start a fire can result in your finished product tasting like petroleum, as the meat absorbs the flavor. If you need help heating things up, try fire starters.

Duke rides high in the saddle in a scene from *The Cowboys* (1972).

RED, WHITE & BLUE SLIDERS

Don't worry—these bite-sized burgers still manage to pack a wallop of flavor.

MAKES 12 SLIDERS

PROVISIONS

TOMATO JAM

2	large tomatoes, chopped
½	cup light brown sugar, packed
2	Tbsp. lemon juice (1 lemon)
2	garlic cloves, minced
1	tsp. ground ginger
1	tsp. kosher or fine sea salt
½	tsp. pepper
½	tsp. ground cloves

BLUE CHEESE BURGERS

1½	lb. ground chuck (80-percent lean)
1	Tbsp. Worcestershire sauce
½	tsp. kosher or fine sea salt
½	tsp. pepper
2	oz. crumbled blue cheese
	Vegetable oil, for grill
12	small potato rolls
½	head iceburg lettuce, shredded

DIRECTIONS

TOMATO JAM

1. Combine all ingredients in a large skillet and cook over medium-high heat.

2. When the tomatoes start to break down and soften, mash with a potato masher.

Continue to boil until the mixture thickens, about 10 minutes. Let cool.

BURGERS

1. Combine all ingredients except vegetable oil, potato rolls and lettuce in a large mixing bowl. Divide the mixture into 12 equal portions. Form into small patties, about 2 inches in diameter, and make an indentation in the middle of each patty with your thumb.

2. Prepare the grill for direct heat and preheat to medium-high. Brush the grates with oil.

3. Grill the burgers 3 to 4 minutes per side with the lid of the grill closed.

4. Place some shredded lettuce on the bottom half of each bun, top with a burger patty, a large dollop of tomato jam and the top half of bun. Secure with picks if desired.

HOT 'N' SPICY SKIRT STEAK

This recipe has two things Duke loved—steak and spice.
We think it will be a favorite for you as well.

SERVES 6

PROVISIONS

SALSA CRIOLLA

- 4 plum tomatoes, seeded and chopped
- 2 red bell peppers, seeded and chopped
- 1 small white onion, finely diced
- 2 garlic cloves, minced
- ¼ cup packed flat leaf parsley leaves, minced
- ½ cup olive oil
- ¼ cup white wine vinegar
- Kosher or fine sea salt and pepper, to taste

STEAK

- 1 cup packed flat leaf parsley
- 1 cup packed basil leaves
- 3 green onions, roughly chopped
- 1 small jalapeño, seeded, deveined and chopped
- 2 garlic cloves, chopped
- ¼ cup olive oil
- 2 Tbsp. white wine vinegar
- 1½ tsp. kosher or fine sea salt
- 1 tsp. pepper
- 2½ lb. skirt steak
- Vegetable oil, for grill

DIRECTIONS

SALSA

1. Combine all ingredients in a mixing bowl. Season to taste with salt and pepper. Cover with plastic wrap and let sit at least 30 minutes at room temperature or in the refrigerator for up to 3 days.

STEAK

1. Place the parsley, basil, green onions, jalapeño, garlic, olive oil, vinegar, salt and pepper in a food processor and process, scraping down the sides a few times, until fully combined and the mixture forms a thick paste.

2. Lay the steaks on a baking sheet and slather on both sides with the herb paste. Cover with plastic wrap and let sit at room temperature for 30 minutes.

3. Prepare the grill for direct heat and preheat to high.

4. Pat the steaks dry with paper towels leaving some of the herbs on the steak. Brush the grates of the grill with oil and cook, with the lid closed, 3 to 4 minutes per side. Let steak rest for 10 minutes before serving. Serve with the salsa.

John Wayne in *Pals of Saddle* (1938).

John Wayne as Ethan Edwards in the Western masterpiece *The Searchers* (1959). Duke appreciated the challenge of portraying the troubled ex-Confederate so much, he named his youngest son Ethan.

COWBOY BURGERS

Like the Ringo Kid or Quirt Evans, these burgers
are an American classic you'll keep revisiting again and again.

SERVES 6

PROVISIONS

- 1½ lb. ground chuck (80-percent lean)
- Vegetable oil, for patties
- Kosher or fine sea salt, to taste
- Freshly ground black pepper, to taste
- ¾ cup barbecue sauce
- 6 slices cheddar or American cheese
- 6 hamburger buns
- 1 (6-oz.) container French fried onions

DIRECTIONS

1. Prepare the grill for direct heat and heat to medium-high.

2. Divide ground chuck into 6 equal portions. Form each portion into patties and make a depression in the center of each patty with your thumb. Brush the patties with oil and season with salt and pepper.

3. Grill the burgers for 4 minutes with lid closed. Brush with barbecue sauce, flip, brush the top of the burger with more sauce, and grill for another 3 minutes. Top each patty with a slice of cheese, close the lid and grill for another minute.

4. Brush both sides of the buns with barbecue sauce. Top the burgers with French fried onions.

DID YOU KNOW?

John Wayne not only turned in another great performance as the lead in *Angel and the Badman*—he also produced the movie, the first time he took on that role.

Duke as Quirt Evans in *Angel and the Badman* (1947).

SIMPLE STRIP STEAK

Nothing brought a smile to Duke's face like a perfect piece of meat.
Cook up this recipe to get you and yours grinning at the dinner table.

SERVES 4

PROVISIONS

STEAKS

4 (8- to 10-oz.) New York strip steaks, 1–1¼ in. thick

Olive oil, for steak

Kosher or fine sea salt, to taste

Pepper, to taste

VINAIGRETTE

4 plum tomatoes, cut in half lengthwise

¼ cup olive oil

1 small shallot, minced

2 Tbsp. red wine vinegar

½ cup packed, fresh basil leaves

Kosher or fine sea salt, to taste

Pepper, to taste

DIRECTIONS

1. Remove the steaks from the refrigerator 30 minutes before grilling. Brush with oil on both sides and season with salt and pepper.

2. Prepare the grill for direct heat, preheating to medium-high.

3. Brush the cut side of the tomatoes with oil and place on the grill. Grill until charred and beginning to soften, about 5 minutes. Remove from the grill and let cool slightly.

4. Chop the tomatoes roughly, removing and discarding the skins as you cut. Place in a bowl along with any juices that accumulate. Add ¼ cup olive oil, the shallot and vinegar and stir to combine. Stir in the basil and season to taste with salt and pepper.

5. Grill the steaks over direct heat with the lid closed 3 to 4 minutes per side for medium rare. Let sit for 10 minutes before slicing.

6. Slice the steaks topped with the vinaigrette.

Duke smiles in one of his classic films.

John Wayne with son Patrick (right) and Chris Mitchum (left) in a scene from *Big Jake* (1971). The movie also featured Duke's youngest son, Ethan.

Duke, Dean Martin, Earl Holliman, and Michael Anderson in *The Sons of Katie Elder* (1965).

BARBECUE BEEF SANDWICHES

These sandwiches are so juicy and tasty,
you'll have no choice but to ask for seconds.

SERVES 8

PROVISIONS

- 1 (3-lb.) boneless beef chuck roast
- 16 slices Texas toast (thickly sliced white bread)
- ½ cup melted butter

BARBECUE SAUCE

- 1 cup ketchup
- ½ cup molasses
- ½ cup honey
- ¾ cup pineapple juice
- 1½ tsp. Worcestershire sauce
- 1 Tbsp. garlic powder
- 1½ tsp. onion powder
- 1 tsp. chipotle chili powder
- ½ tsp. black pepper
- ½ tsp. kosher salt
- 6 dashes Tabasco sauce

QUICK PICKLED RED ONIONS

- 1 cup warm water
- ½ cup apple cider vinegar
- 1 Tbsp. sugar
- 1½ tsp. kosher or fine sea salt
- 1 medium red onion, cut in half and thinly sliced

DIRECTIONS

BARBECUE SAUCE

1. Combine all the ingredients in a large saucepan and whisk well. Bring to a boil over high heat. Once it begins to boil, reduce heat and simmer, stirring occasionally, for 30 minutes or until the sauce is thick and glossy. Let cool.

PICKLED RED ONIONS

1. Whisk the water, vinegar, sugar and salt together until the sugar and salt dissolve.

2. Place the onions in a bowl or mason jar, pour the vinegar water solution over, mix, cover and let sit at room temperature for 1 hour or in the refrigerator for up to a week.

BEEF

1. Cut the roast in half and place in a 3–4 quart slow cooker. Reserve 1 cup barbecue sauce, refrigerate covered, and pour the rest into the slow cooker. Cover and cook on low 8 to 10 hours or until the beef is very tender. Remove the meat and let cool slightly. Drain the cooking liquid from the slow cooker.

2. Using 2 forks, shred the beef. Return to the slow cooker, add the reserved 1 cup barbecue sauce, cover and cook for another 15 to 20 minutes or until heated through.

3. Position the top rack of oven 4 to 6 inches from the heat source and pre-heat the broiler to high.

4. Toast the Texas toast on both sides under the broiler until golden brown. Brush melted butter on one side of each piece. Spoon about 1 cup of the beef on the buttered side of one piece of toast, top with some pickled red onions, and place another piece of toast, buttered side down, on top.

SOUTH OF THE BORDER BURGERS

Like many of Duke's characters, these spicy burgers reflect the rich cultural melting pot of the West.

SERVES 6

PROVISIONS

- 1½ lb. ground chuck (80-percent lean)
- 1 (10-oz.) can tomatoes and chilies, drained
- Vegetable oil, for patties
- Kosher or fine sea salt, to taste
- Pepper, to taste
- 6 slices pepper jack cheese
- 6 hamburger buns
- 2 ripe avocados
- 1 lime, juiced
- Salsa (see recipe on page 28 or use store-bought Chunky Salsa)
- 6 hamburger buns

DIRECTIONS

1. Prepare the grill for direct heat and heat to medium-high.

2. In a large mixing bowl, combine the meat with the drained tomatoes and chilies. Divide into 6 equal portions. Form each portion into patties and make a depression in the center of each patty with your thumb. Brush the patties with oil and season with salt and pepper.

3. Grill the burgers for 4 minutes with the lid closed. Flip and grill for another 3 minutes. Top each patty with a slice of cheese, close the lid and grill for another minute. Toast the buns lightly on the grill.

4. Mash the avocados with lime juice and salt and pepper to taste.

5. Serve the burgers on buns topped with the mashed avocado and salsa.

Duke with his oldest son Michael.

DID YOU KNOW?

Mexico was one of John Wayne's favorite vacation destinations. He even owned part of a luxury hotel in Acapulco, Hotel Los Flamingos, where he could kick back in style.

Plain and Tasty
Pork Chops,
Page 102

THE WHOLE HOG

★

THE OTHER WHITE MEAT IS A BBQ STAPLE.

BARBECUE PORK TENDERLOINS

Treat yourself to some first-rate tenderloin tonight. You've earned it.

SERVES 6

PROVISIONS

- ½ cup barbecue sauce
- ½ cup orange marmalade
- ¼ cup ketchup
- 2 Tbsp. Sriracha sauce
- 2 Tbsp. Worcestershire sauce
- 1 tsp. garlic powder
- 2 (1 ¼-lb.) pork tenderloins

DIRECTIONS

1. Combine the barbecue sauce, marmalade, ketchup, Sriracha, Worcestershire sauce and garlic powder in a medium mixing bowl and mix well. Pour half the sauce into a large food storage bag, add the pork tenderloins, squeeze out excess air and refrigerate for 1 to 12 hours. Place the rest of the sauce in a small bowl, cover and refrigerate until ready to grill the pork. Remove the pork from refrigerator, discard the marinade and let sit at room temperature for 15 to 20 minutes.

2. Prepare grill for direct heat and preheat to medium-high. Grill the pork for 10 to 12 minutes or until it reaches an internal temperature of 140 degrees F, turning every 2 minutes.

3. Place the tenderloins on a piece of foil, brush with half the remaining sauce, wrap and let sit for 5 minutes before slicing. Serve the rest of the sauce on the side.

Maureen O'Hara and John Wayne in *McLintock!*, 1963.

DID YOU KNOW?

In several interviews, Maureen O'Hara has fondly recalled cooking for both her husband and her frequent costar, John Wayne. The meals often consisted of meat and potatoes.

CHISUM'S CHILI-BRINED PORK CHOPS

Only the toughest gunslingers can handle the spice in these chops—but the taste is worth the struggle.

SERVES 4

PROVISIONS

- 4   center cut pork loin chops about 1 in. thick
- Vegetable oil, for chops
- Pepper, to taste

BRINE

- 3   cups warm water
- ¼   cup kosher salt
- ¼   cup agave nectar or honey
- 4   Tbsp. lime juice (from 2 limes)
- 1   jalapeño pepper, sliced
- 3   cups ice

TOMATILLO SALSA

- 6   tomatillos
- 1   jalapeño pepper
- 6   green onions
- ½   cup cilantro leaves

DIRECTIONS

BRINE

1. Combine the warm water with the salt, agave, lime juice and jalapeño pepper and stir until the salt has dissolved. Add the ice and stir until the mixture is cool.

2. Pour the brine mixture into a large food storage bag. Add the pork chops, squeeze out the air from the bag and seal. Place in the refrigerator for 2 to 12 hours.

3. Remove from refrigerator, discard the brine, rinse the pork with cold water and let sit at room temperature for 15 to 20 minutes. Brush with oil and season with pepper.

4. Prepare grill for direct heat and indirect heat and preheat to medium-high.

SALSA

1. Remove the husk from the tomatillos. Place the tomatillos, jalapeño and green onions on the grill over direct heat. Grill, turning occasionally, until charred and soft, about 4 minutes for the green onions and 10 for the tomatillos and jalapeño.

2. Cut the stem off the jalapeño and scrap off the skin. Place in a food processor with the tomatillos and onion. Process until almost smooth. Add the cilantro and pulse several times.

PORK

1. Grill the chops for 3 minutes over direct heat, flip and grill for another 3 minutes. Move the chops to the indirect heat side of the grill and grill with the lid closed for another 7 to 8 minutes, turning once or until an internal temperature of 140 degrees F is reached. Serve with the salsa.

DID YOU KNOW?

The ranch house that was used in John Wayne's 1970 film *Chisum* can be seen again in his film *Big Jake*, which was released just one year later in 1971.

John Wayne in a scene from the 1970 film *Chisum*.

CHILI-RUBBED PORK TENDERLOINS

A great cut of pork seasoned in a savory rub
is the right way to end a long day.

SERVES 4

PROVISIONS

1   (1¼- to 1½-lb.) pork tenderloin

CHILI RUB

1½ tsp. chili powder

½ tsp. ground cumin

½ tsp. garlic powder

½ tsp. kosher or fine sea salt

¼ tsp. pepper

CORN AND AVOCADO SALSA

1½ tsp. chili powder

½ tsp. ground cumin

1   cup frozen corn kernels, thawed

1   large tomato,
     seeded and chopped

1   avocado, diced

½ cup diced red onion

½ cup cilantro leaves

2   Tbsp. lime juice (from 1 lime)

DIRECTIONS

RUB

1. Combine all rub ingredients together in a small bowl.

2. Rub seasoning all over the pork. Wrap in plastic wrap and refrigerate for 30 minutes to 8 hours. Remove pork from refrigerator 20 minutes before grilling.

SALSA

1. Combine all salsa ingredients in a small bowl. Refrigerate covered until serving time.

PORK

1. Prepare grill for direct heat and preheat to medium-high. Grill the pork for 10 to 12 minutes or until it reaches an internal temperature of 140 degrees F, turning every 2 minutes.

2. Let pork sit 5 to 10 minutes before slicing. Serve with salsa.

DID YOU KNOW?

To prepare for filming of *The Undefeated*, John Wayne had to lose all of the weight he had intentionally gained to play Rooster Cogburn in 1969's *True Grit*.

Duke surveys cattle in a scene from *McLintock!* (1963). The movie, which costarred Maureen O'Hara, was a loose adaptation of Shakespeare's *The Taming of the Shrew*.

BANDITO PORK BURGERS

These burgers are so tasty, they should be outlawed!

SERVES 4

PROVISIONS

QUICK AVOCADO AIOLI

- 1   ripe avocado
- 1   garlic clove, minced
- 1   Tbsp. lime juice
- ¼   cup mayonnaise

CHIPOTLE BURGERS

- 1   lb. ground pork
- ½   cup grated Monterey Jack cheese
- 1   chipotle pepper in adobo sauce, minced plus 2 tsp. of sauce
- 1   tsp. kosher or fine sea salt
- ½   tsp. pepper
- 4   hamburger buns
- 4   slices tomato
- 4   slices red onion

DIRECTIONS

QUICK AVOCADO AIOLI

1. Mash the avocado in a small mixing bowl with the garlic and lime juice. Add the mayonnaise and combine well. Cover and refrigerate until serving time.

CHIPOTLE BURGERS

1. Prepare grill for direct heat and preheat to medium-high.

2. Combine the pork, cheese, chipotle pepper and sauce, salt and pepper in a medium mixing bowl. Divide the mixture into 4 equal portions, shape into patties and make a deep impression with your thumb in the center of each patty. Brush the grill grates with oil and grill the patties with the lid closed 4 to 5 minutes per side.

3. Spread some aioli on the bottom half of the bun, top with tomato, onion, pork burger, another dollop of aioli and the top half of the bun.

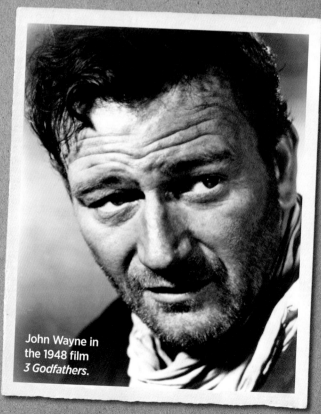

John Wayne in the 1948 film *3 Godfathers*.

84

WAYNE FAMILY TIP

You may be used to ordering your beef burgers medium-rare, but pork's a whole different beast (literally). Make sure your pork burgers are cooked all the way before enjoying.

WAYNE FAMILY TIP

If you decide to add extra herbs
and spices of your choice to this
recipe, aim to add just a hint
of flavor as it can be easy to
overpower the pork.

SALOON-STYLE BRINED PORK

Once you serve this sweet and salty dish, your guests will be tipping their hats to you.

SERVES 4

PROVISIONS

BRINE

3 cups warm water

½ cup kosher salt

½ cup sugar

½ cup orange juice (from 2 large oranges)

2 bay leaves

3 cups ice

1 (1½-lb.) pork tenderloin

Vegetable oil, for tenderloin

Pepper, to taste

ORANGE MUSTARD

½ cup orange marmalade

1½ Tbsp. Dijon mustard

1 tsp. honey

½ tsp. garlic powder

DIRECTIONS

BRINE

1. Combine the warm water with the salt, sugar, orange juice and bay leaves. Stir until sugar and salt have dissolved. Add the ice and stir until the mixture is cool.

2. Pour the brine mixture into a large food storage bag. Add the pork tenderloin, squeeze out the air from the bag and seal. Place in the refrigerator for 2 to 12 hours. Remove from refrigerator, discard the brine, rinse the pork with cold water and let sit at room temperature for 15 to 20 minutes. Brush with oil and season with pepper.

PORK

1. Prepare grill for direct heat and preheat to medium-high. Grill the pork for 10 to 12 minutes or until it reaches an internal temperature of 140 degrees F, turning every 2 minutes. Cover with foil and let sit for 5 minutes before slicing.

ORANGE MUSTARD

1. Combine all ingredients and mix well. Serve with the pork.

John Wayne in *The Man Who Shot Liberty Valance*, 1962.

GRILLED PORK TENDERLOIN SALAD

Dress up your greens with a big, juicy helping of pork. You'll thank us later.

SERVES 4

PROVISIONS

TENDERLOIN

- ⅓ cup olive oil
- 4 Tbsp. lemon juice (from 1 lemon)
- 1 tsp. dried oregano
- 1 tsp. garlic powder
- 1 tsp. onion powder
- 1 (1- to 1 ½-lb.) pork tenderloin

CREAMY GREEK DRESSING

- ½ cup Greek yogurt
- ¼ cup sour cream
- ¼ cup olive oil
- 4 Tbsp. lemon juice (from 1 lemon)
- 1 Tbsp. minced fresh dill
- 1 garlic clove, minced
- 1 tsp. dried oregano
- Kosher or fine sea salt, to taste
- Pepper, to taste

SALAD

- 4 cups chopped romaine lettuce hearts
- 2 tomatoes, chopped
- 1 seedless cucumber, thinly sliced
- ½ small red onion, diced
- ½ cup crumbled feta cheese
- ¼ cup pitted Kalamata olives

DIRECTIONS

TENDERLOIN

1. Combine the olive oil, lemon juice, oregano, garlic powder and onion powder in a small mixing bowl. Pour into a large food storage bag, add the pork tenderloin, squeeze out the air, seal the bag and let marinate at room temperature for 30 minutes or in the refrigerator for up to 8 hours.

DRESSING

1. Whisk all ingredients together well in a small mixing bowl. Season to taste with salt and pepper. Cover and refrigerate until serving time. Can be made up to 3 days in advance.

2. Prepare grill for direct heat and preheat to medium-high.

3. Remove the pork from the marinade and discard the marinade. Pat dry. Brush the grill grates with vegetable oil and grill the pork with the lid closed, turning every two minutes, for about 12 minutes or until it reaches an internal temperature of 140 degrees F. Remove from grill and let sit 5 minutes before slicing.

SALAD

1. Combine the salad ingredients in a large mixing bowl. Pour in about ⅓ of the dressing and toss to coat. Place the salad on a platter. Slice the tenderloin, place on top of the salad and serve with the remaining dressing on the side.

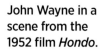

John Wayne in a
scene from the
1952 film *Hondo*.

HONDO'S HAM STEAK

Whether you're working on the ranch or riding dispatch for the cavalry, this hefty steak will settle your hunger.

SERVES 3 TO 4

PROVISIONS

- 1   (1- to 1½-lb.) ham steak
- 2   Tbsp. butter
- 1   Tbsp. flour
- ½   cup strong brewed coffee
- ½   cup water
- 1   tsp. sugar
  Kosher or fine sea salt, to taste
  Pepper, to taste

DIRECTIONS

1. Prepare grill for direct heat and preheat to medium-high. Brush the grate and grill the ham steak 3 to 4 minutes per side with the lid open.

2. In a medium skillet, melt the butter. Add the flour and cook, stirring, for 1 minute. Add the coffee, water and sugar and cook, stirring, until thickened, about 3 minutes. Season to taste with salt and pepper but do not over-salt as the ham is already salty.

3. Serve the ham with the gravy.

WAYNE FAMILY TIP

If you want to serve your ham steaks with those iconic grill lines, simply throw the steaks on the grill and only touch them when they need to be flipped.

91

PROSPECTOR'S PORK BURGERS

If you've been looking for a burger with the perfect touch of sweetness, you've hit the motherlode.

SERVES 4

PROVISIONS

QUICK APPLE CHUTNEY

- 1 Tbsp. butter
- 2 apples, cored and chopped
- 3 Tbsp. brown sugar
- 2 Tbsp. apple cider vinegar
- ½ tsp. dried ginger

PORK BURGERS

- 1 lb. ground pork
- 1 tsp. garlic powder
- 1 tsp. kosher or fine sea salt
- ½ tsp. dried sage
- ½ tsp. pepper
- Vegetable oil, for grill
- 4 biscuits or hamburger buns

DIRECTIONS

CHUTNEY

1. In a medium skillet, melt the butter over medium. Add the apples, brown sugar, vinegar and ginger and stir to combine. Cook the apples, uncovered, stirring occasionally until tender, about 8 minutes. Raise the heat to high and cook, stirring, for another minute or two until all the liquid has evaporated. Let cool.

BURGERS

1. Prepare grill for direct heat and preheat to medium-high.

2. Combine the pork, garlic powder, salt, sage and pepper in a medium mixing bowl. Divide the mixture into 4 equal portions, shape into patties and make a deep impression with your thumb in the center of each patty. Brush the grill grates with oil and grill the patties with the lid closed 4 to 5 minutes per side.

3. Place some of the apple chutney on the bottom half of each biscuit or bun, top with a pork burger, a large dollop of chutney and finally the top half of the biscuit or bun.

John Wayne in *North to Alaska*, 1960.

DID YOU KNOW?

In one scene from *North to Alaska*, John Wayne's character searches for a man in a bar while a version of a song called "North to Alaska" plays in the background.

DONOVAN'S HAWAIIAN KEBOBS

John Wayne loved making movies and memories in the Aloha State,
and these kebobs will make you feel like you're in the islands.

MAKES 6 SKEWERS

PROVISIONS

- 1 (1- to 1¼-lb.) pork tenderloin
- 1 (20-oz.) can pineapple chunks
- 3 Tbsp. soy sauce
- 3 Tbsp. brown sugar
- ½ tsp. garlic powder
- ½ tsp. dried ginger
- ¼ tsp. kosher or fine sea salt
- 2 red bell peppers
- Vegetable oil, for grill

DIRECTIONS

1. Cut the pork into 24 (1-in.) pieces. Drain the can of pineapple, reserving ¼ cup of the juice.

2. Combine the pineapple juice with the soy sauce, brown sugar, garlic powder, ginger and salt in a medium mixing bowl. Pour the mixture into a large food storage bag, add the pork, seal the bag and let sit at room temperature for 20 to 30 minutes, flipping the bag occasionally.

3. Prepare the grill for direct heat and pre-heat to medium-high.

4. Drain the pork and discard the marinade. Cut the peppers into 24 chunks. Thread the skewers alternating pork and peppers with pineapple chunks.

5. Brush the grates of the grill with oil and grill the skewers for about 12 minutes, turning every 2 minutes.

John Wayne, Lee Marvin and Elizabeth Allen in *Donovan's Reef*, 1963.

WAYNE FAMILY TIP

Kebobs can be tricky when you're grilling a variety of foods on the same skewer. Instead, try threading each skewer with just one ingredient—pork with pork, peppers with peppers, etc. Once cooked, remove and let guests choose what they want.

Duke shares a scene with George "Gabby" Hayes in 1934's *Blue Steel*. Hayes made a career playing the colorful sidekick for many Western stars including Duke, Roy Rogers and Randolph Scott.

BACKCOUNTRY SAUSAGE SANDWICHES

Even the most buttoned-up city slicker will be doing backflips after a bite of these sandwiches.

SERVES 6

PROVISIONS

- 2 Tbsp. olive oil
- 1 medium white or yellow onion, thinly sliced
- 1 red bell pepper, seeded, deveined and thinly sliced
- 1 green bell pepper, seeded, deveined and thinly sliced
- 1 tsp. kosher or fine sea salt
- ½ tsp. pepper
- 6 Italian sausages
- 6 hoagie rolls

DIRECTIONS

1. Heat oil in a large skillet over medium-high. Add the onion and cook, stirring occasionally, until soft, about 5 minutes. Add the peppers, salt and pepper and cook, stirring occasionally, until the peppers are soft and the vegetables are starting to brown, about 10 minutes. Keep warm.

2. Prepare the grill for direct heat and preheat to medium-high.

3. Prick the sausages with a fork in several places to keep them from bursting. Grill for 10 to 12 minutes, turning every 2 minutes, with the lid closed or until browned on the outside and juices run clear.

4. Serve the sausages on hoagie rolls topped with onions and peppers.

John Wayne in the 1932 film *The Big Stampede*

GREAT PLAINS RIBS

These lip-smackin' ribs will hold a special place in your heart even as they fill your stomach.

PROVISIONS

- 2 racks pork baby back ribs

  Kosher or fine sea salt, to taste

  Pepper, to taste

BARBECUE SAUCE

- 2 Tbsp. olive oil
- 1 small white onion, very finely diced
- 2 cups ketchup
- ½ cup molasses
- ½ cup brown sugar, packed
- ½ cup apple juice
- ½ cup apple cider vinegar
- 2 Tbsp. paprika
- 1 Tbsp. garlic powder
- 1 tsp. kosher or fine sea salt
- 1 tsp. black pepper

  Hot sauce, to taste

  Vegetable oil, for grill

DIRECTIONS

RIBS

1. Preheat oven to 250 degrees F.

2. Flip the ribs bone side up and insert a dinner knife just under the white membrane that covers the meat and bones. Gently peel the membrane off. Generously season with salt and pepper.

3. Wrap ribs in foil, place on a baking sheet and bake in oven for 2 hours 30 minutes to 3 hours or until the ribs are tender.

BARBECUE SAUCE

1. Heat oil in a medium saucepan over medium-high. Add the onions and cook, stirring occasionally, until tender, about 5 minutes. Add the ketchup, molasses, brown sugar, apple juice, vinegar, paprika, garlic powder, salt and pepper. Bring mixture to a gentle boil, reduce heat and simmer, uncovered, for 30 to 40 minutes. Add hot sauce to taste. Remove from heat and let cool.

2. When ribs are tender, prepare grill for direct heat and preheat to medium. Oil the grill grates.

3. Remove the ribs from the foil, slather with barbecue sauce and grill over direct heat 5 to 7 minutes per side, basting every 2 minutes with barbecue sauce. Serve any remaining sauce on the side.

George Hayes and John Wayne in *Dark Command* (1940).

DID YOU KNOW?

Dark Command (1940), which sees Duke cast as the marshal of Lawrence, Kansas, was the first film the legend made after his breakout role in *Stagecoach* (1939).

PLAIN AND TASTY PORK CHOPS

Like a cowboy hat on Duke's head, these chops are going to look right at home on your dinner table.

SERVES 4

PROVISIONS

½ cup plus 2 Tbsp. maple syrup, divided

½ cup kosher salt

3 Tbsp. plus 1 tsp. Dijon mustard, divided

2 Tbsp. fresh rosemary, minced

1 tsp. pepper, plus more to taste

2 cups water

4 cups ice

4 center-cut loin pork chops (about 1 in. thick)

Vegetable oil, for chops

Duke in *The War Wagon* (1967).

DIRECTIONS

1. Combine ½ cup maple syrup, salt, 3 Tbsp. Dijon mustard, rosemary and 1 tsp. pepper with the water in a saucepan. Bring to a boil, stirring to dissolve the salt. Take off the heat, stir in the ice. Pour the brining liquid into a large plastic storage bag. Add the chops, squeeze out the air, close the bag and refrigerate for between 1 and 12 hours.

2. Remove from refrigerator, discard the brine, rinse the pork with cold water and let sit at room temperature for 15 to 20 minutes. Brush with oil and season with pepper.

3. Prepare grill for direct heat and indirect heat and preheat to medium-high. Combine the remaining 2 Tbsp. maple syrup with the remaining 1 tsp. of Dijon mustard.

4. Grill the chops for 3 minutes over direct heat, flip and grill for another 3 minutes. Move the chops to the indirect heat side of the grill and grill with the lid closed for another 7 to 8 minutes, turning once, or until an internal temperature of 140 degrees F is reached. Brush the chops with the maple/mustard sauce. Let chops sit for 5 minutes before serving.

WAYNE FAMILY TIP

You don't want to put chops dripping with brine directly on the grill, as your meat will steam rather than sear. Avoid this by patting the chops dry with a paper towel.

SOUTHERN-STYLE RIBS

A rack of ribs is to barbecue as John Wayne is to Westerns—hard to beat.

SERVES 6

PROVISIONS

- 2 racks pork baby back ribs
- Vegetable oil, for grill

RUB

- ¼ cup dark brown sugar, packed
- ¼ cup paprika
- 1 Tbsp. kosher or fine sea salt
- 1 Tbsp. pepper
- 1 Tbsp. onion powder
- 1 Tbsp. garlic powder
- 2 tsp. dry mustard
- 2 tsp. cayenne pepper

DIRECTIONS

1. Mix all rub ingredients together in a small mixing bowl.

2. Flip the ribs bone side up and insert a dinner knife just under the white membrane that covers the meat and bones. Gently peel the membrane off. Reserve ¼ of the rub mixture and coat the ribs with the rest. Wrap in foil and refrigerate 4 to 8 hours.

3. Preheat oven to 250 degrees F. Keep the ribs wrapped in foil, place on a baking sheet and bake in oven for 2 hours 30 minutes to 3 hours or until the ribs are tender.

4. Prepare the grill for direct heat and preheat to medium-high. Oil the grill grates. Remove the ribs from the foil, sprinkle with the reserved rub mixture and grill 7 to 10 minutes per side.

John Smith, Duke and Claudia Cardinale in *Circus World* (1964).

DID YOU KNOW?

Filming for *Circus World* (1964) took place in Europe, which gave Duke the perfect excuse to enjoy time on the *Wild Goose*! The actor and his family enjoyed the waters near Spain.

PARADISE CANYON PORK CHILI VERDE

Don't accept a counterfeit version of this classic—this recipe is the real deal.

SERVES 6 TO 8

PROVISIONS

- 2 tsp. ground cumin
- 1½ tsp. kosher or fine sea salt
- 1 tsp. pepper
- 2 lb. pork tenderloin
- 2 Tbsp. olive or vegetable oil
- 1 large white or yellow onion, diced
- 4 garlic cloves, minced
- 1 jalapeño pepper, deveined, seeded and minced
- 1½ lb. tomatillos, husk removed, rinsed and chopped
- 2 tsp. smoked paprika
- 4 cups vegetable or chicken stock
- 2 cups cilantro leaves, divided
- 1 bunch green onions, trimmed and roughly chopped
- 1 lb. Yukon gold potatoes, diced
- 1 lime, juiced

  Lime wedges and corn tortillas for serving

DIRECTIONS

1. Combine the cumin, salt and pepper in a medium mixing bowl. Cut the tenderloin into 1-in. pieces and add to the spice mixture. Toss well to coat.

2. Heat the oil in a large stock pot or Dutch oven over medium-high. Add the pork and cook, stirring occasionally, until the pork is browned on all sides, about 6 to 8 minutes. Remove the pork from the pot, place in a bowl and set aside. Add the onions and cook, stirring occasionally, until softened and starting to brown, about 5 minutes. Add the garlic and jalapeño and cook, stirring for 1 minute. Add the tomatillos, oregano and paprika and cook, stirring occasionally, until the tomatillos soften, about 5 minutes. Return the pork along with any juices that have accumulated back into the pot.

3. Combine the stock, 1½ cups cilantro and the green onions in a blender and puree. Pour the mixture into the pot, bring to a boil, reduce heat, cover and simmer for 30 minutes. Add the potatoes and simmer another 30 minutes or until the pork and potatoes are fork tender. Add the lime juice and adjust seasoning with more salt and pepper if needed. Just before serving, stir in the remaining ½ cup cilantro leaves.

4. Serve with lime wedges and corn tortillas.

Duke and Yakima Canutt in *Paradise Canyon* (1935).

WAYNE ✕ **FAMILY**

TIP

When it comes to cooking your pork, you want to put safety first. Insert an instant-read thermometer into the thickest part of the meat and make sure the meat is at least 145 degrees F.

PATRIOT PORK RIBS

Celebrate your American pride the John Wayne way with this hefty and hearty rib roast.

SERVES 6 TO 8

PROVISIONS

- 1 (4- to 5-lb.) bone-in center cut pork loin roast

  Pepper, to taste

  Vegetable oil, for grill

BRINE

- ½ cup maple syrup
- ½ cup kosher salt
- ½ cup apple cider vinegar
- 2 Tbsp. minced rosemary
- 3 cups warm water
- 3 cups ice

MAPLE MUSTARD SAUCE

- ¼ cup maple syrup
- ¼ cup spicy brown mustard
- 1 Tbsp. lemon juice

Duke in *The Horse Soldiers* (1959).

DIRECTIONS

BRINE

1. Combine maple syrup, salt, vinegar, rosemary and warm water in a large mixing bowl and stir until the salt has dissolved. Add the ice and stir until cool. Add the pork roast, cover with plastic wrap and refrigerate for 12 hours. Remove from refrigerator and let sit for 1 hour before grilling.

PORK

1. Prepare grill for direct and indirect heat and preheat to medium.

2. Remove pork from brine, rinse with cold water, pat dry and season on all sides with pepper. Brush the grill grates with oil.

3. Grill over direct heat 5 minutes per side. Move to indirect heat and grill with the lid closed 45 to 60 minutes or until the pork reaches an internal temperature of 145 degrees F.

MUSTARD SAUCE

1. While pork is cooking, combine all sauce ingredients in a small bowl and stir well to combine.

2. When pork is done, brush with some of the mustard sauce, cover with foil and let sit for 10 minutes before slicing between the bones.

3. Serve remaining sauce on the side.

Duke flying high in his plane en route to the 26 Bar Ranch. Although the actor loved the time he spent in Arizona, he left the day-to-day management of the ranch to Louis Johnson, who could dedicate the time needed for such a task.

PROSCIUTTO WRAPPED GRILLED PORK

What's the only way to make a pork dish better? Add more pork.

SERVES 4

PROVISIONS

APPLE COMPOTE

- 1 Tbsp. butter
- 2 large apples, cored and chopped
- ¼ cup dried cherries or cranberries
- 2 Tbsp. sugar
- ¼ tsp. kosher or fine sea salt
- 2 Tbsp. balsamic vinegar

PORK

- 1 (1- to 1 ½-lb.) pork tenderloin
  Garlic powder, to taste
  Pepper, to taste
- 6 oz. prosciutto, very thinly sliced
  Vegetable oil, for grill

DIRECTIONS

APPLE COMPOTE

1. In a medium saucepan over medium heat, melt the butter. Add the apples, cherries or cranberries, sugar and salt. Toss to coat. Cover the pot and cook gently for about 15 minutes or until the apples and cherries or cranberries are tender. Remove the lid, raise the heat and bring the mixture to a boil. Add the vinegar and cook, stirring, until all liquid has evaporated. Let cool. Can be made up to a week in advance. Store covered in the refrigerator. Let come to room temperature before serving.

PORK

1. Prepare the grill for direct and indirect heat and preheat to medium.

2. Sprinkle all sides of pork with garlic powder and pepper. Lay the prosciutto slices next to each other on a cutting board. Place the tenderloin on top of the prosciutto and fold the prosciutto over pressing firmly. Brush grill grates with oil. Place the pork over direct heat and grill about 3 minutes per side or until the prosciutto is crispy. Move the pork to the indirect side of the grill and grill with the lid closed for another 10 to 12 minutes or until the pork reaches an internal temperature of 140 degrees F. Let sit for 5 minutes before slicing.

3. Serve the pork with the compote.

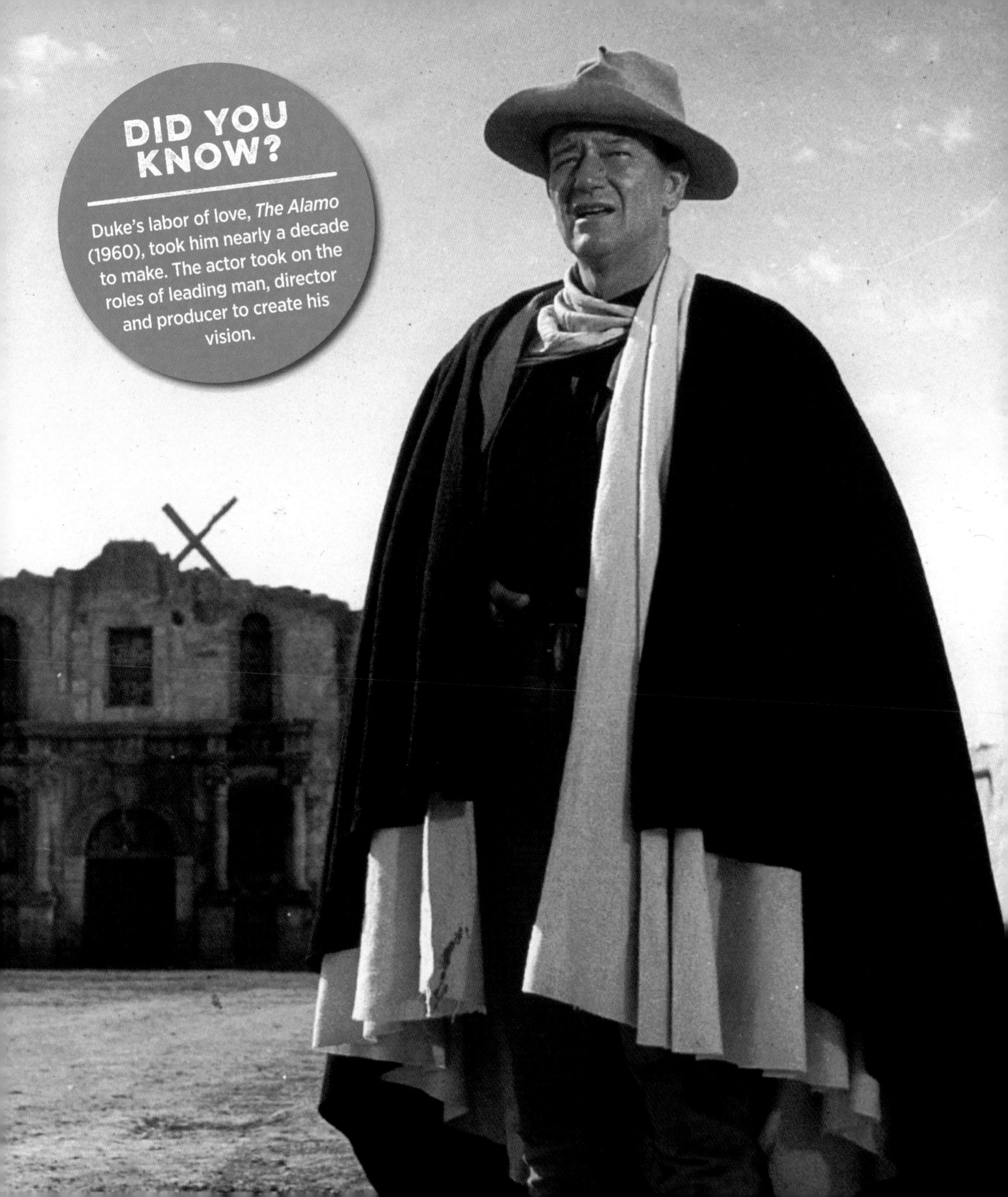

DID YOU KNOW?

Duke's labor of love, *The Alamo* (1960), took him nearly a decade to make. The actor took on the roles of leading man, director and producer to create his vision.

PULLED PORK NACHOS

These nachos will open your eyes (or eye) to a new world of deliciousness.

SERVES 6 TO 8

PROVISIONS

- **6** oz. corn tortilla chips
- **2** cups warmed Pulled Pork (see page 119)
- **2** cups grated cheddar cheese
- **½** cup quick pickled red onions (see page 71), drained
- **¼** cup pickled jalapeño pepper slices, drained

DIRECTIONS

1. Position oven rack about 6 in. from the top. Preheat broiler to high.

2. Place tortilla chips on a heatproof platter or in a cast iron skillet. Top with pulled pork and cheese. Broil until the cheese is melted, 2 to 3 minutes.

3. Top with pickled red onions and pickled jalapeño pepper slices.

John Wayne in *True Grit* (1969).

DID YOU KNOW?

John Wayne may continue to stand tall as America's most beloved actor, but the legend only has a single Oscar to his name—a Best Actor award for his work in *True Grit*.

PONY EXPRESS PULLED PORK SANDWICHES

Grab one of these mouth-watering sammies to keep you full on the go.

SERVES 8

PROVISIONS

4–5 cups hot Pulled Pork (see recipe page 119)

8 hamburger buns or Kaiser rolls, lightly toasted or grilled

COLESLAW

1 small head green cabbage or 1 (16-oz.) bag coleslaw mix

¼ cup mayonnaise

2 Tbsp. apple cider vinegar

1 Tbsp. sugar

1 tsp. kosher or fine sea salt

½ tsp. pepper

DIRECTIONS

1. Combine all coleslaw ingredients in a medium mixing bowl. Cover and refrigerate for 30 minutes for best flavor or serve immediately.

2. Place a heaping ½ cup of pulled pork on the bottom bun, top with coleslaw and top bun.

John Wayne looking tough and hungry.

Duke in *The Big Stampede* (1932).

DID YOU KNOW?

John Wayne didn't just play a cowboy in the movies—he also owned a livestock ranch in Arizona. Every year around Thanksgiving, he would host a large cattle sale.

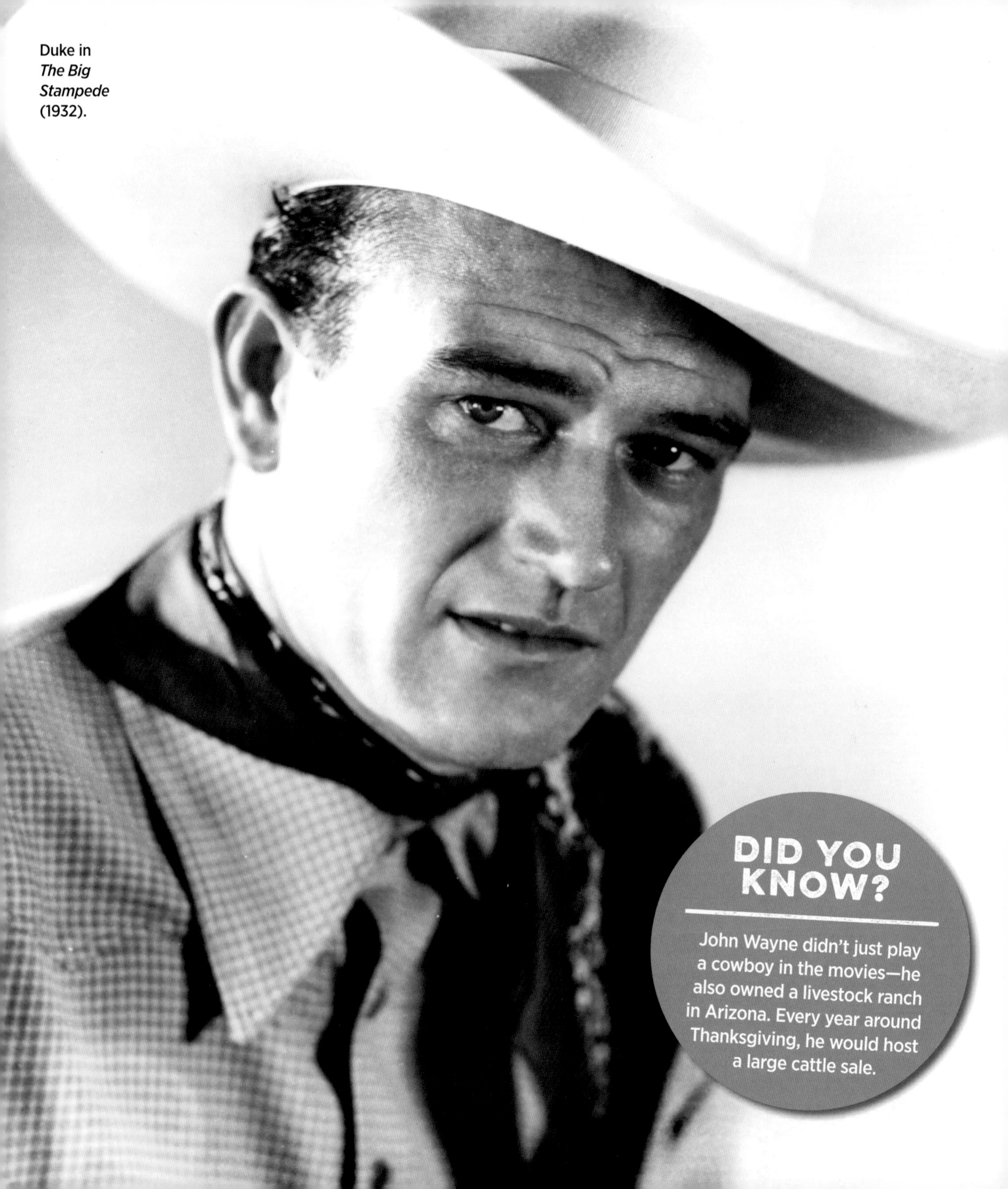

BIG 'N' TASTY PULLED PORK

Don't you dare let anyone tell you one helping is enough of this recipe.

SERVES 8 TO 10

PROVISIONS

Vegetable oil, for slow cooker

1   (5- to 6-lb.) pork butt roast

2   cups cola

PORK RUB

½   cup brown sugar

¼   cup sugar

¼   cup kosher salt

2   Tbsp. chili powder

2   tsp. onion powder

2   tsp. garlic powder

2   tsp. paprika

1   tsp. pepper

BARBECUE SAUCE

1   cup cola (not diet)

1   cup ketchup

¼   cup Worcestershire sauce

2   Tbsp. apple cider vinegar

2   Tbsp. pork rub

DIRECTIONS

RUB

1. Combine all rub ingredients in a small bowl. Reserve 2 Tbsp. for the sauce. Rub the rest of the seasoning on the pork.

PORK

1. Lightly grease a 6-lb. slow cooker with oil. Place the pork roast in the slow cooker, add 2 cups cola, cover and cook on low for 8 to 10 hours.

BARBECUE SAUCE

1. Combine all ingredients and 2 Tbsp. of rub in a medium sauce pan. Bring to a boil over medium heat. Reduce heat and simmer gently, stirring occasionally, for 6 to 8 minutes or until slightly reduced. Let cool. Can be made ahead and stored in the refrigerator, covered, for up to 2 weeks.

2. When the pork is done, remove from the slow cooker and drain the cooking liquid. Shred the pork with 2 forks, return to slow cooker along with the barbecue sauce. Cook on low, covered, for about 15 minutes or until heated through.

John Wayne delivers a knockout blow in a scene from *Red River Range* (1938). Duke once defined the ideal man as someone "never looking for a fight but never backing down from one either."

SPICY SAUSAGE CHEESE BURGERS

These burgers really pack a punch—and a kick.

SERVES 4

PROVISIONS

PEPPER COMPOTE

- 1 Tbsp. olive oil
- 1 small white onion, finely diced
- ½ red bell pepper, seeded and finely chopped
- ½ green bell pepper, seeded and finely chopped
- ½ tsp. kosher or fine sea salt
- ¼ tsp. pepper

BURGERS

- 1 lb. loose breakfast or Italian sausage
  Vegetable oil, for patties
- 4 slices cheddar cheese
- 1 stick butter, at room temperature
- 2 garlic cloves, minced
- 4 hamburger rolls

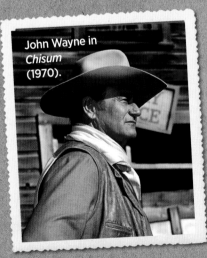

John Wayne in *Chisum* (1970).

DIRECTIONS

PEPPER COMPOTE

1. In a medium skillet over medium-high, heat the oil. Add the onion, peppers, salt and pepper and cook, stirring occasionally, until the vegetables are soft and starting to brown, about 10 minutes. Reserve until serving time.

BURGERS

1. Prepare the grill for direct and indirect heat and preheat to medium.

2. Divide the sausage into 4 equal portions, shape into patties, and make a deep impression with your thumb in the center of each patty. Brush the patties with oil, and grill over direct heat with the lid closed 4 to 5 minutes per side. Place a slice of cheese on top of each burger 1 minute before done and cook with lid closed until the cheese starts to melt, about 1 minute.

3. Position top oven rack 6 in. from top and preheat the broiler to high.

4. Combine the butter and garlic. Spread both halves of the hamburger buns. Place the buns on a baking sheet, cut side up and broil until toasted, about 1 to 2 minutes.

5. Serve the sausage burgers on the garlic toasted buns topped with pepper compote.

EL DORADO PORK SKEWERS

Whether you're a sheriff, a rancher or just a meat-loving American, these pork skewers are sure to satisfy.

MAKES ABOUT 24 SKEWERS

PROVISIONS

- 2 Tbsp. paprika
- 1 Tbsp. ground cumin
- 2 tsp. garlic powder
- 1 tsp. ground coriander
- 1 tsp. dried oregano
- 1 tsp. kosher or fine sea salt
- ½ tsp. pepper
- ¼ cup olive oil
- 2 Tbsp. lemon juice
- 2 lb. pork tenderloin, cut into 1-in. pieces
- 24 wooden skewers, soaked in water for ½ hour
- Vegetable oil, for grill

DIRECTIONS

1. Combine the paprika, cumin, garlic powder, coriander, oregano, salt and pepper in a medium mixing bowl and stir well to combine. Add the olive oil and lemon juice and stir well. Pour into a large food storage bag, add the pork, squeeze out the air, seal the bag and refrigerate for 2 to 12 hours.

2. Prepare the grill for direct heat and preheat to medium-high.

3. Thread 2 to 3 pieces of pork on each skewer.

4. Brush the grill grates with oil and grill the skewers for about 3 minutes per side or until browned and cooked through.

DID YOU KNOW?

John Wayne didn't just work with one member of the Mitchum family. In addition to starring with Robert Mitchum, Duke shared the screen with the actor's son Chris in several films.

John Wayne and Robert Mitchum in *El Dorado* (1966).

BARBECUED BIRDS

THERE'S NOTHING "FOWL" ABOUT THESE DISHES.

Conqueror's Chicken Wings, Page 139

GUN-SMOKEY BARBECUE CHICKEN

Help yourself to some high-caliber chicken with this recipe.

SERVES 4 TO 6

PROVISIONS

- 3 Tbsp. melted butter
- ¼ cup plus 3 Tbsp. Worcestershire sauce, divided
- 1 (3½- to 4-lb.) whole chicken, cut into 8 pieces
- Kosher or fine sea salt, to taste
- Pepper, to taste
- Vegetable oil, for grill
- 1 cup ketchup
- ½ cup brown sugar
- ½ cup honey
- ¼ cup apple cider vinegar
- 1½ tsp. garlic powder
- 1½ tsp. onion powder

DIRECTIONS

1. Prepare the grill for direct and indirect heat and preheat to medium.

2. Combine the melted butter with 3 Tbsp. Worcestershire sauce and brush liberally on all sides of the chicken pieces. Season well with salt and pepper. Brush the grill grates with oil.

3. Place the chicken pieces skin side up on the indirect side of the grill placing the smaller pieces farthest away from the heat source. Grill for 20 minutes with the lid closed. Flip the chicken pieces, close the lid and grill for another 20 minutes or until the internal temperature reaches 160 degrees F.

4. While the chicken is grilling, combine the ketchup, brown sugar, honey, remaining ¼ cup Worcestershire sauce, apple cider vinegar, garlic powder and onion powder in a small saucepan. Bring to a boil over medium-high heat. Reduce heat and simmer for 10 minutes. Let cool.

5. When the chicken reaches 160 degrees F, brush with the sauce and move to the direct heat side of the grill. Cook for 4 to 5 more minutes, brush with sauce, flipping every minute or two. Serve any remaining sauce on the side.

John Wayne on the television show *Gunsmoke*, 1955.

HOME ON THE RANGE CHICKEN

This crispy, juicy bird will have everyone running to the table—no dinner bell needed.

SERVES 4

PROVISIONS

- 1 cup Italian parsley
- ¼ cup cilantro leaves
- ½ cup olive oil
- ¼ cup white wine vinegar
- 1 tsp. dried oregano
- 1 tsp. kosher or fine sea salt
- ½ tsp. pepper
- ½ tsp. red pepper flakes
- 8 boneless, skinless chicken thighs
- Vegetable oil, for grill

DIRECTIONS

1. Place the parsley, cilantro, olive oil, vinegar, oregano, salt, pepper and red pepper in a blender and process until well blended, scraping down the sides as needed. Place ½ cup in a covered container and refrigerate until serving time. Pour the rest into a large food storage bag, add the chicken thighs, squeeze out the excess air, seal the bag and refrigerate 1 to 12 hours.

2. Prepare the grill for direct heat and preheat to medium-high.

3. Remove chicken from the bag, discarding any marinade. Brush the grill grates with oil and grill for 4 to 5 minutes per side or until the internal temperature reaches 160 to 165 degrees F.

4. Serve the chicken with the reserved sauce.

John Wayne and Montgomery Clift in *Red River*, 1948.

DID YOU KNOW?

Despite shooting in Arizona, the crew of *Red River* experienced several downpours. Unphased, John Wayne convinced director Howard Hawks to work the weather into the script.

SOUTHWESTERN SADDLEBAG CHICKEN

Round up these ingredients and you've got a great packet of protein to go.

SERVES 6

PROVISIONS

- 4 boneless, skinless chicken breasts
- 1 cup fresh or frozen (thawed) corn kernels
- 1 (15-oz.) can black beans, rinsed and drained
- 1 red bell pepper, seeded, deveined and chopped
- ½ cup chunky salsa
- 1 cup grated cheddar cheese

DRY RUB

- 2 Tbsp. chili powder
- 1 tsp. ground cumin
- 1 tsp. kosher or fine sea salt
- ½ tsp. pepper
- ¼ tsp. garlic powder
- ¼ tsp. onion powder

DIRECTIONS

1. Prepare grill for direct heat and preheat to medium.

2. Combine all the rub ingredients together in a small bowl.

3. Rub the chicken breasts with rub and let sit at room temperature for a few minutes while preparing the vegetables.

4. Combine the corn, black beans and bell pepper in a bowl and mix well.

5. Place four 18- by 12-in. pieces of foil on a work surface and spray each piece with cooking spray. Divide the vegetable mixture evenly in the center of each piece of foil.

6. Slice the chicken breasts into ½-in. strips and lay on top of the vegetables. Top the chicken with the salsa. Seal the foil bundles well. Place on the grill and grill for 15 to 20 minutes or until the chicken is no longer pink inside. Carefully unwrap the foil packets, divide the cheese evenly among the packets on top of the chicken, reseal the packets and let sit for 2 minutes to let the cheese melt.

Riders of Destiny, 1933

DID YOU KNOW?

Aware that his talents did not include crooning, John Wayne was happy to have director Robert N. Bradbury's son dub the singing scenes in 1933's *Riders of Destiny.*

CONQUEROR'S CHICKEN WINGS

With their fierce flavor, these wings are sure to take over any table.

SERVES 6 TO 8

PROVISIONS

- 1 Tbsp. kosher or fine sea salt
- 1 Tbsp. paprika
- 1 Tbsp. garlic powder
- 1½ tsp. onion powder
- 1½ tsp. cayenne pepper
- 1½ tsp. dried oregano
- 1½ tsp. black pepper
- 1½ tsp. dried thyme
- ⅓ cup olive oil
- 3 lb. chicken wings
- Vegetable oil, for grill
- ¼ cup butter
- ¼ cup hot sauce
- 1 Tbsp. Worcestershire sauce

DIRECTIONS

1. Combine the herbs and spices with the olive oil. Pour into a large food storage bag, add the chicken wings, squeeze out the excess air, seal and refrigerate for 2 to 12 hours, turning the bag occasionally.

2. Prepare grill for direct heat and preheat to medium-high. Remove the chicken wings from the marinade, discarding the marinade. Brush the grill grates with oil. Grill the wings with the lid closed 8 minutes per side or until the chicken is cooked through and the wings are golden brown.

3. While the wings are grilling, combine the butter, hot sauce and Worcestershire sauce. Cook over medium heat until the butter has melted. Stir the mixture well and pour into a large mixing bowl. Add the cooked wings and toss to coat in the sauce.

John Wayne as Genghis Khan in *The Conqueror*, 1956.

DID YOU KNOW?

John Wayne was a huge fan of Asian artwork and furniture. His home, while filled with the Western works one would expect, also featured many Eastern pieces.

In a scene from *The Cowboys* (1972), Duke's Wil Andersen watches his young charges wolf down a meal. John Wayne himself enjoyed spending mealtime with his family, and his youngest son Ethan remembers those shared moments as special times of togetherness.

WILD WEST CHICKEN AND CHEDDAR BURGERS

The original burger is an American classic, but this daring dish gives it a run for its money.

SERVES 4

PROVISIONS

- 1½ lb. ground chicken
- Vegetable oil, for patties
- Kosher or fine sea salt, to taste
- Pepper, to taste
- 4 slices cheddar cheese
- 4 hamburger buns
- Mayonnaise
- 4 lettuce leaves
- 8 slices tomatoes
- 4 slices onion

DIRECTIONS

1. Prepare the grill for direct heat and heat to medium-high.

2. Divide the chicken into 4 equal-sized portions. Form each portion into patties and make a depression in the center of each patty with your thumb. Brush the patties with oil and season with salt and pepper.

3. Grill the burgers for 4 minutes with the lid closed. Flip and cook another 3 minutes, top each patty with a slice of cheese, close the lid and grill for another minute or until the burgers are cooked through and the cheese melts.

4. Lightly grill the hamburger buns. Spread some mayonnaise on each side of the bun. Serve the burgers on the buns with lettuce, tomato and onion.

DID YOU KNOW?

The desert region of Monument Valley, Utah, was the filming location of many of John Wayne's movies—including the film considered to be his first big break, *Stagecoach* (1939).

WAYNE FAMILY TIP

If you're hosting a hungry crowd for a summer cookout, serve these skewers with the Star Packer Potato Salad on page 215. Any meal of meat and potatoes is one John Wayne would approve of.

CHISUM'S CHICKEN AND CHORIZO SKEWERS

Saddle up—these skewers will take you on a wild ride of flavor.

MAKES 20 TO 24 SKEWERS

PROVISIONS

20–24 wooden skewers

4 Tbsp. olive oil

2 Tbsp. lemon juice

2 garlic cloves, minced

2 tsp. paprika

1 tsp. kosher or fine sea salt

½ tsp. pepper

2 lb. boneless, skinless chicken thighs, cut into 1-in. pieces

2 lb. Spanish or Portuguese chorizo

2 white onions

Vegetable oil, for grill

2 cups arugula

2 lemons, cut into wedges for serving

DIRECTIONS

1. Soak the skewers in water for 30 minutes.

2. Combine the olive oil, lemon juice, garlic, paprika, salt and pepper in a mixing bowl. Add the cut up chicken thighs, toss to coat and let marinate for 15 to 20 minutes.

3. Prepare the grill for direct heat and preheat to medium-high.

4. Slice the chorizo into ¼-in. rounds.

5. Cut the onions in half horizontally, then cut each half into 6 wedges.

6. Alternate chorizo, chicken and a few slices of onion on the skewers, threading about 4 of each on each skewer. Brush the grill grates with vegetable oil and grill 8 to 10 minutes with the lid closed, turning the skewers every 2 minutes.

7. Serve the skewers on a bed of arugula with lemon wedges.

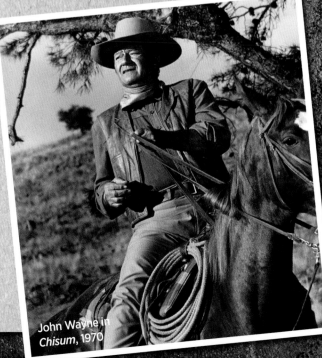

John Wayne in *Chisum*, 1970

COMANCHERO CHICKEN FAJITA BURGERS

Once your friends and family have a taste of these burgers,
they might just steal the recipe like a band of thieves.

SERVES 4

PROVISIONS

- 1 Tbsp. olive oil
- 1 medium white onion, thinly sliced
- 1 green bell pepper, seeded, deveined and thinly sliced
- 1 red bell pepper, seeded, deveined and thinly sliced
- ½ tsp. kosher or fine sea salt
- ¼ tsp. pepper
- 2 ripe avocados
- ¼ cup chunky salsa
- 1 lime, juiced
- 1½ lb. ground chicken
- ½ cup grated cheddar cheese
- 4 hamburger buns

DIRECTIONS

1. Heat the oil in a large skillet over medium-high. Add the onion, peppers, salt and pepper, and cook, stirring occasionally, until softened and starting to brown, about 8 minutes. Remove from the pan and set aside.

2. Mash the avocados with the salsa and lime juice and season to taste with salt and pepper.

3. Prepare the grill for direct heat and heat to medium-high.

4. Combine the chicken and cheese in a large mixing bowl. Divide into 4 equal-sized portions. Form each portion into patties and make a depression in the center of each patty with your thumb. Brush the patties with oil and season with salt and pepper.

5. Grill the burgers for 4 minutes with the lid closed. Flip and cook another 4 minutes or until the burgers are cooked through.

6. Serve the burgers on buns spread with the avocado mixture and topped with the onion and pepper mixture.

Duke with Ina Balin in
The Comancheros, 1961.

NO-PUNCHES-PULLED CHICKEN

John Wayne could trade fisticuffs with the best of 'em, and this
chicken is a satisfying smack in the tastebuds.

SERVES 8

PROVISIONS

- 1 (3½- to 4-lb.) whole chicken, cut into 8 pieces
- 4 cups chicken stock or water
- 1 (15-oz.) can dark sweet cherries, undrained
- 1 cup ketchup
- ¾ cup pineapple juice
- 1 Tbsp. Worcestershire sauce
- 1 Tbsp. garlic powder
- 1 Tbsp. onion powder
- 1 tsp. (more if you like it spicier) chipotle chili powder
- 8 hamburger buns, toasted
  McClintock Coleslaw (see page 194)

DIRECTIONS

1. Place the chicken in a saucepan or Dutch oven with the chicken stock or water. Bring to a boil, cover the pot, reduce heat to a simmer and cook until the chicken is cooked through, about 20 to 25 minutes. Remove the chicken from the liquid, let cool enough to handle then remove the skin and bones. Discard skin and bones and shred the chicken.

2. Puree the cherries along with their liquid in a blender and blend until smooth. Pour into a large saucepan and add the ketchup, pineapple juice, Worcestershire sauce, garlic, onion and chipotle chili powder. Stir to combine. Bring to a boil, reduce heat and simmer, uncovered, until thickened to the consistency of barbecue sauce, about 30 minutes. Add the shredded chicken to the sauce, stirring to combine.

3. Serve on hamburger buns with a scoop of cilantro lime slaw.

Duke in the 1970 film, *Chisum*.

DID YOU KNOW?

The realistic fist fighting seen in many of John Wayne's movies is a Hollywood technique that was created by Duke and rodeo world champion Yakima Canutt.

OLD-FASHIONED BARBECUE CHICKEN PIZZA

Like seeing "John Wayne" on a movie poster, the appeal of this dish is right in the name.

SERVES 2 TO 4

PROVISIONS

Flour for rolling the dough

1 lb. pre-made pizza dough

Cornmeal

2 cups No-Punches-Pulled Chicken (see page 145)

½ cup barbecue sauce, divided

8 oz. fresh mozzarella cheese, sliced

¼ small red onion, thinly sliced

½ cup fresh cilantro leaves

DIRECTIONS

1. Prepare the grill for direct heat and preheat to high.

2. Flour a work surface and roll the dough into a circle or rectangle. Sprinkle a generous layer of cornmeal in a flat baking sheet or pizza paddle. Place the rolled out dough on top.

3. Combine the chicken with ¼ cup barbecue sauce. Spread the remaining ¼ cup on the dough. Place the sliced mozzarella on the sauce, top with chicken and red onions.

4. Brush the grill grates with vegetable oil. Grill pizza for 4 to 5 minutes with the lid closed or until dough is brown and cheese is melted. Top with cilantro and serve.

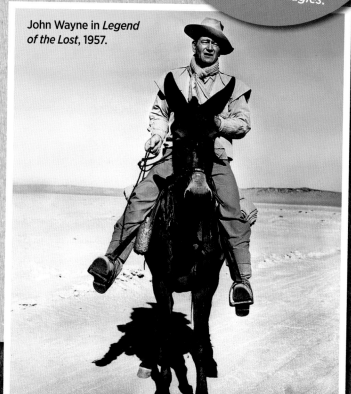

DID YOU KNOW?

The year 1957 was a particularly busy one for John Wayne. The always-busy icon starred in three films that year: *Legend of the Lost*, *Jet Pilot* and *The Wings of Eagles*.

John Wayne in *Legend of the Lost*, 1957.

RIO LOBO CHICKEN BREASTS

After you try this chicken, you'll be lassoing seconds in no time.

SERVES 4

PROVISIONS

- 4 boneless, skinless chicken breasts
- 1 cup cilantro
- ½ cup olive oil
- 1 jalapeño pepper, seeded, deveined and roughly chopped
- 4 Tbsp. fresh lime juice (from 2 limes)
- 1 Tbsp. honey
- 1 tsp. kosher or fine sea salt
- 1 tsp. ground cumin
- ½ tsp. pepper
-    Vegetable oil, for grill
-    Lime wedges for serving

DIRECTIONS

1. Place a piece of waxed paper on a work surface, top with one chicken breast and another piece of waxed paper. Using a rolling pin, pound the chicken breast until it is about ½-in. thick. Repeat with remaining chicken breasts. Place the chicken breasts in a 9- by 12-in. baking dish.

2. Place the cilantro, olive oil, jalapeño pepper, lime juice, honey, salt, cumin and pepper in a blender and process until smooth. Reserve a quarter of the marinade and pour the rest over the chicken breasts, making sure to coat each one well on both sides. Cover with plastic wrap and refrigerate for 30 minutes to 12 hours.

3. Prepare the grill for direct heat and preheat to medium-high.

4. Remove the chicken from the dish, discarding the marinade. Brush the grill grates with oil and grill 3 minutes per side or until the internal temperature reaches 160 to 165 degrees F. Remove the chicken from the grill and immediately brush with the reserved marinade. Serve with lime wedges if desired.

Rio Lobo, 1970

WAYNE FAMILY TIP

Don't like white meat? Feel free to swap the chicken breasts with thighs or drumsticks. Just be sure to adjust cooking time as necessary.

Duke is all smiles in a scene from *The Undefeated* (1969). The film was the only time John Wayne shared the screen with Rock Hudson, another actor who made his mark on the Western genre.

SOUTHERN SUN CHICKEN WINGS

These wings are packed with finger-lickin' citrus flavor that's sure to ignite appetites.

SERVES 4 TO 6

PROVISIONS

- ½ cup olive oil
- 4 Tbsp. lemon juice
- 2 Tbsp. lime juice
- ½ cup Italian parsley, chopped (measure then chopped)
- 2 garlic cloves, minced
- 1 Tbsp. minced fresh rosemary (measured then minced)
- 1 tsp. kosher or fine sea salt
- ½ tsp. pepper
- 2 lb. chicken drumettes
- Vegetable oil, for grill

DIRECTIONS

1. Combine all ingredients except chicken drumettes and vegetable oil in a mixing bowl and whisk well to combine. Pour into a large food storage bag, add the chicken wings, squeeze out the excess air and seal. Refrigerate for 2 to 12 hours, turning the bag occasionally.

2. Prepare grill for direct heat and preheat to medium-high. Remove the chicken wings from the marinade, discarding the marinade. Brush the grill grates with oil. Grill the wings 8 minutes per side or until the chicken is cooked through and the wings are golden brown.

The Alamo, 1960

MEDITERRANEAN GRILLED CHICKEN

A world traveler, Duke's favorite part of vacation was trying the local grub.
Make like the legend and expand your palate.

SERVES 4

PROVISIONS

4 boneless, skinless chicken breasts

MARINADE

¼ cup olive oil

2 Tbsp. lemon juice (from 1 lemon)

1 tsp. dried oregano

½ tsp. kosher or fine sea salt

¼ tsp. pepper

YOGURT DILL SAUCE

¾ cup Greek yogurt

¼ cup sour cream

2 Tbsp. minced fresh dill

½ tsp. kosher or fine sea salt

½ tsp. pepper

Vegetable oil, for grill

DIRECTIONS

MARINADE

1. Combine all the marinade ingredients together in a small bowl. Pour into a large food storage bag. Add the chicken breasts, squeeze out the excess air, seal the bag, and refrigerate for 1 to 12 hours.

YOGURT DILL SAUCE

1. Combine all the sauce ingredients together in a small bowl. Cover with plastic wrap and refrigerate until serving time. Can be made a day ahead.

CHICKEN

1. Prepare the grill for direct heat and preheat to medium-high.

2. Remove the chicken from the bag, discard the marinade and pat the chicken dry with paper towels.

3. Brush the grill grates with oil and grill with the lid closed for 6 to 8 minutes per side or until the chicken reaches an internal temperature of 165 degrees F.

4. Serve the chicken breasts with the sauce.

RISERVATO

Duke enjoying himself in Italy.

DID YOU KNOW?

John Wayne loved a homemade meal, but he also enjoyed the local eateries in the towns he visited. One of his favorite spots was Bob Taylor's Ranch House in Las Vegas.

John Wayne and Al Ferguson in *The Desert Trail*, 1935.

WAYNE FAMILY TIP

Some people have an aversion to cilantro, so you may want to have an alternative on hand when serving these tacos. Lettuce, particularly bibb lettuce, works well as a replacement.

DESERT TRAIL CHICKEN TACOS

It's no mirage—these delicious tacos are real and soon to leave you delighted.

SERVES 4

PROVISIONS

CHICKEN

- 1 tsp. ground cumin
- 1 tsp. kosher or fine sea salt
- ½ tsp. pepper
- 1 lb. boneless, skinless chicken thighs
- Olive oil, for chicken

SALSA

- 1 lb. husked tomatillos
- 1 jalapeño pepper
- 1 small white or yellow onion, thickly sliced
- Vegetable oil, to taste
- 1 cup fresh cilantro leaves
- 4 Tbsp. lime juice (from 2 limes)
- 1 avocado
- Kosher or fine sea salt, to taste
- Pepper, to taste

FOR SERVING

- 8 corn tortillas
- 1 avocado, sliced
- 1 tomato, sliced
- Cilantro leaves
- Lime wedges

DIRECTIONS

1. Prepare the grill for direct heat and preheat to medium-high.

2. Combine the cumin, salt and pepper in a small bowl. Brush the chicken thighs with olive oil and coat generously with the seasoning. Let sit at room temperature while preparing the salsa.

3. Coat the whole tomatillos, jalapeño pepper and onion slices with vegetable oil and place on the grill. Grill with the lid closed for 10 minutes, or until the vegetables are charred and soft, turning the vegetables a few times while cooking. Remove from grill and let cool slightly.

4. Cut the avocado in half, remove the seed but leave the peel on. Brush the cut sides with oil and place on the grill, cut side down, for 2 minutes or just until charred slightly.

5. Remove the stem from the jalapeño pepper and place in a blender with the tomatillos, onion slices and lime juice. Process until the salsa is chunky. Scoop out the flesh from the avocado and add to the blender with the cilantro. Pulse a few times to combine. Season to taste with salt and pepper.

6. Place the chicken thighs on the grill and cook with the lid closed 4 minutes per side or until cooked through. Let chicken rest for 5 minutes before slicing or chopping.

7. Lightly grill the tortillas.

8. Serve the tortillas with the chicken, salsa, avocado, tomato slices, cilantro leaves and lime wedges.

MANGO-TOPPED CHICKEN BREASTS

John Wayne once said, "A man oughta do what he thinks is right."
In this case, covering chicken with downright delicious salsa fits the bill.

SERVES 4

PROVISIONS

DRY RUB

- 2 tsp. chili powder
- 1 tsp. ground cumin
- 1 tsp. kosher or fine sea salt
- ½ tsp. pepper
- ½ tsp. cayenne pepper
- ¼ tsp. garlic powder
- ¼ tsp. onion powder
- Olive oil, for grill
- 4 boneless, skinless chicken breasts

MANGO SALSA

- 2 ripe mangos, chopped
- ½ small red onion, finely diced
- ½ cup fresh cilantro
- 1 small jalapeño pepper, seeded, deveined and minced
- 4 Tbsp. lime juice
- Vegetable oil, to taste

DIRECTIONS

MANGO SALSA

1. Combine all the salsa ingredients together in a small bowl. Cover with plastic wrap and refrigerate until serving time. Can be made a day ahead.

2. Prepare the grill for direct heat and preheat to medium-high.

DRY RUB

1. Combine all the rub ingredients together in a small bowl.

CHICKEN

1. Brush the chicken breasts with olive oil and apply the rub liberally on all sides. Can be grilled immediately or covered and placed in the refrigerator for up to 12 hours.

2. Brush the grill grates with oil and grill with the lid closed for 6 to 8 minutes per side or until the chicken reaches an internal temperature of 165 degrees F.

3. Serve the chicken breasts with the salsa.

Tall in the Saddle, 1944

WAYNE FAMILY TIP

If you want to add just a little more sweetness to your salsa, try switching out the red onion for a Vidalia onion. Prepare the same way you would the red onion.

GRILLED CHICKEN CAESAR SALAD

You won't regret digging into this mouthwatering salad for dinner.

SERVES 6

PROVISIONS

- 2 tsp. garlic powder
- 2 tsp. kosher or fine sea salt
- 1 tsp. pepper
- Olive oil, for chicken
- 4 boneless, skinless chicken breasts
- 1 baguette
- Vegetable oil, for brushing
- 2 heads romaine lettuce
- 1 pint cherry tomatoes, halved
- ½ cup grated Parmesan cheese

DRESSING

- ¾ cup olive oil
- 1 Tbsp. mayonnaise
- 1 tsp. Dijon mustard
- 2 garlic cloves, minced
- ¼ cup lemon juice
- 1 tsp. kosher or fine sea salt
- ½ tsp. pepper
- ¼ cup grated Parmesan cheese

DIRECTIONS

1. Prepare the grill for direct heat and preheat to medium-high.

2. Whisk the dressing ingredients together in a small bowl. Cover and refrigerate until serving time. Can be made a day ahead.

3. Combine the garlic powder, salt and pepper in a small bowl. Brush the chicken breasts with olive oil and apply the seasoning generously on all sides.

4. Cut the baguette in half lengthwise and brush both cut sides well with olive oil.

5. Grill the chicken with the lid closed for 6 to 8 minutes per side or until they reach an internal temperature of 160 degrees F. Put on a plate and let cool. Grill the bread with the lid open until lightly charred, about 2 minutes.

6. Chop the chicken and romaine lettuce. Place in a salad bowl with the tomatoes. Add the dressing and toss. Cut the bread into bite-sized pieces and add to the salad with ½ cup Parmesan cheese. Toss and serve.

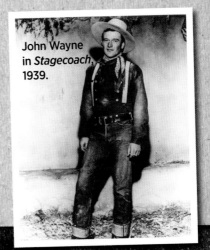

John Wayne in *Stagecoach*, 1939.

STRAIGHT SHOOTER STUFFED PEPPERS

Like Duke himself, these peppers get right to the point with no unnecessary fanfare.

SERVES 6

PROVISIONS

- 8 oz. cream cheese, at room temperature
- 2 cups cooked chicken, shredded
- ½ cup salsa (see page 28 or use store-bought Chunky Salsa) plus more for serving
- ¾ tsp. kosher or fine sea salt
- ½ tsp. pepper
- 3 large bell peppers, red, yellow, green or a combination
- Vegetable oil, for grill
- ¾ cup grated cheddar cheese
- Sour cream, to serve

DIRECTIONS

1. Prepare the grill for indirect heat and preheat to medium.

2. Combine the cream cheese, chicken, ½ cup salsa, salt and pepper in a large mixing bowl and mix well.

3. Cut bell peppers in half lengthwise and scrape out the seeds. Stuff the chicken mixture into the peppers packing it in lightly. Brush the grill grates with oil and grill with the lid closed for 10 to 12 minutes or until the peppers are soft. Divide the cheese evenly among the peppers and grill with the lid closed for another minute or two or until the cheese melts.

4. Serve with sour cream and salsa.

DID YOU KNOW?

The gun John Wayne is most frequently seen wielding in his Western films is an 1873 Colt Single Action Army pistol, which is also commonly known as a Colt Peacemaker.

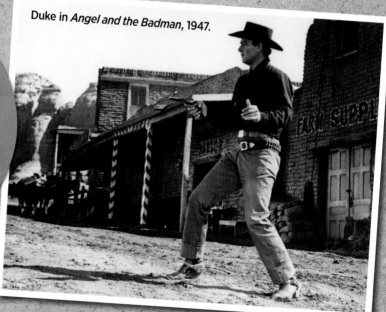

Duke in *Angel and the Badman*, 1947.

John Wayne as Big Jake in the 1971 film. *Big Jake* also starred sons Patrick and Ethan, making the movie a family affair.

TEXAS TURKEY LEGS

Next time you've got an appetite the size of the Lone Star state, fire up these tasty turkey drumsticks.

SERVES 4

PROVISIONS

- 1   tsp. kosher or fine sea salt
- 1   tsp. pepper
- 1   tsp. garlic powder
- 1   tsp. onion powder
- 4   turkey legs
- Vegetable oil, for grill
- ¼   cup ketchup
- 2   Tbsp. brown sugar
- 1   Tbsp. soy sauce
- ½   Tbsp. lemon juice
- 1   tsp. hot sauce

DIRECTIONS

1. Prepare the grill for direct and indirect heat and preheat to medium.

2. Combine the salt, pepper, garlic powder and onion powder in a small bowl. Brush the turkey legs with oil and sprinkle the spice mixture all over.

3. Brush grill grates with oil. Grill the turkey legs over direct heat 5 minutes per side then move to indirect heat and grill with the lid closed for 30 minutes.

4. Combine the ketchup, brown sugar, soy sauce, lemon juice and hot sauce in a small saucepan and bring to a boil.

5. After turkey legs have grilled over indirect heat for 30 minutes, brush with the sauce and turn every couple minutes, brush with more sauce each time you turn them. Continue to cook for another 10 minutes or until they reach an internal temperature of 165 degrees F. Baste one last time with sauce and serve hot.

Duke in *The Alamo*, 1960.

DID YOU KNOW?

Despite often being associated with the Lone Star state, John Wayne only made three films in Texas: 1956's *The Searchers*, 1960's *The Alamo* and 1968's *Hellfighters*.

RANCHER'S FAVORITE CHICKEN

This is the meal you want to come home to after a hard day's work.

SERVES 6

PROVISIONS

- ½ cup orange marmalade
- ½ cup olive oil
- 1 tsp. kosher salt
- ½ tsp. freshly ground black pepper
- 1¼–1½ tsp. chipotle chili powder, divided
- 12 boneless, skinless chicken thighs, trimmed of any excess fat
- 3 medium oranges, peeled and chopped
- ½ medium red onion, diced
- 2 plum tomatoes, seeded and chopped
- ¼ cup fresh cilantro, roughly chopped
- 1 lime, juiced
-    Vegetable oil, for grill

DIRECTIONS

1. In a small mixing bowl, whisk together marmalade, olive oil, salt, pepper and 1 tsp. chipotle chili powder. Pour into a large food storage bag. Add the chicken thighs and marinate at room temperature for 1 hour or overnight in the refrigerator.

2. In a medium mixing bowl, combine chopped oranges, red onion, tomatoes, cilantro, lime juice and ¼–½ tsp. chipotle chili powder (depending on how spicy you want it). Reserve.

3. Heat grill to medium-high and brush the grates with oil. Remove the chicken from marinade and discard the marinade. Pat chicken dry and grill covered for 6 to 8 minutes per side. Serve with the citrus salsa.

Duke in *Tall in the Saddle*, 1944

WAYNE FAMILY TIP

This chicken dish will cover your fruit bases pretty well, but if you want to complete the meal even more by serving vegetables on the side, try mashed potatoes and grilled asparagus.

SOUTHWESTERN TURKEY BURGERS

You'd be a turkey not to gobble down these burgers by the plateful.

SERVES 4

PROVISIONS

- ½ cup mayonnaise
- 1 Tbsp. Sriracha sauce
- 1½ lb. ground turkey
- ½ cup grated cheddar cheese
- Vegetable oil, for patties
- Kosher or fine sea salt, to taste
- Pepper, to taste
- 4 hamburger buns
- 1 avocado, sliced

DIRECTIONS

1. Combine the mayonnaise and Sriracha sauce in a small bowl. Refrigerate, covered until ready to serve.

2. Prepare the grill for direct heat and heat to medium-high.

3. Combine the turkey and cheese in a large mixing bowl. Divide into 4 equal-sized portions. Form each portion into patties and make a depression in the center of each patty with your thumb. Brush the patties with oil and season with salt and pepper.

4. Grill the burgers for 4 minutes with the lid closed. Flip and cook another 4 minutes or until the burgers are cooked through.

5. Lightly grill the hamburger buns. Spread some spicy mayonnaise on each side of the bun. Serve the burgers on the buns with avocado slices.

John Wayne in the 1939 film *New Frontier.*

WAYNE FAMILY TIP

To ensure you're buying ripe avocados, give them a little squeeze. If it feels like a stone, it needs a few days to ripen. If it almost explodes, it's too far gone. But if it gives just a little under pressure, take it to the checkout counter.

WESTERN BACON CHICKEN SKEWERS

When it came to grilling, Duke always believed the more meat, the better.

MAKES 6 SKEWERS

PROVISIONS

- 1 lb. boneless, skinless chicken breasts cut into 1-in. pieces
- 12 slices Canadian bacon, cut into quarters
- ½ pint cherry tomatoes

  Vegetable oil, for grill

MARINADE

- ½ cup mayonnaise
- ¼ cup buttermilk
- 1 Tbsp. lemon juice (from 1 lemon)
- ½ tsp. garlic powder
- ½ tsp. onion powder
- ½ tsp. kosher or fine sea salt
- ¼ tsp. pepper

CHIVE AIOLI

- ½ cup mayonnaise
- 1 garlic clove, minced
- 2 Tbsp. chopped chives

DIRECTIONS

MARINADE

1. Combine the mayonnaise, buttermilk, lemon juice, garlic powder, onion powder, salt and pepper in a small mixing bowl and whisk well. Pour the mixture into a large food storage bag, add the chicken, squeeze out the excess air, seal the bag and refrigerate for 1 to 12 hours.

CHIVE AIOLI

1. Combine the mayonnaise, garlic and chives in a small bowl and whisk well. Cover with plastic wrap and refrigerate until serving time. Can be made a day ahead.

CHICKEN

1. Prepare the grill for direct heat and preheat to medium-high.

2. Remove chicken from the bag, discarding the marinade, and pat dry. Alternate the chicken on skewers with the Canadian bacon and tomatoes.

3. Brush the grill grates with oil and grill the skewers for 10 to 12 minutes with the lid closed, turning the skewers every 2 minutes.

4. Serve the skewers with the aïoli.

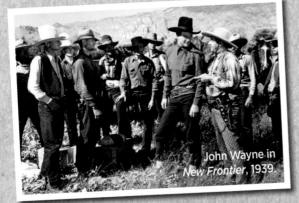

John Wayne in *New Frontier*, 1939.

WAYNE FAMILY TIP

If you're looking to save some time, you can make the process of mixing the chive aioli a little quicker by mixing the ingredients in a food processor or a blender rather than by hand.

John Wayne in the 1949 film *The Fighting Kentuckian*.

DID YOU KNOW?

John Wayne and Oliver Hardy's comedic chemistry in *The Fighting Kentuckian* is one of only two examples of Hardy appearing in a film without his partner, Stan Laurel.

FRONTIERSMAN'S FINGER-LICKIN' KICKIN' CHICKEN

This recipe packs quite a wallop of flavor, so the faint of heart need not apply.

SERVES 6

PROVISIONS

Olive oil, for chicken

6 bone-in, skin-on chicken breasts

DRY RUB

2 Tbsp. chili powder

2 tsp. kosher or fine sea salt

2 tsp. garlic powder

1½ tsp. cayenne pepper

1 tsp. pepper

½ tsp. dried cumin

ALABAMA WHITE SAUCE

1 cup mayonnaise

2 Tbsp. apple cider vinegar

1 Tbsp. prepared horseradish

2 tsp. sugar

1 tsp. kosher or fine sea salt

½ tsp. pepper

Vegetable oil, for grill

DIRECTIONS

ALABAMA WHITE SAUCE

1. Whisk all ingredients together in a small mixing bowl. Cover with plastic wrap and refrigerate until ready to serve. Can be prepared up to 3 days in advance.

DRY RUB

1. Combine all rub ingredients together in a small bowl.

CHICKEN

1. Brush the chicken wings with olive oil and liberally season with the dry rub. Place chicken in a large food storage bag, squeeze out excess air, seal and refrigerate for 1 to 12 hours.

2. Prepare the grill for indirect heat and preheat to medium. Brush the grill grates with oil. Place the chicken on the grill skin side down and grill with lid closed for 15 minutes. Flip the chicken over and grill for another 15 to 20 minutes with the lid closed or until the chicken reaches an internal temperature of 160 to 165 degrees F.

3. Serve the chicken with the sauce.

John Wayne helps set up a shot for *True Grit* (1969) with producer Hal Wallis standing behind the legend. Wallis, who was behind classics such as *Casablanca* (1942), also produced the sequel to *True Grit*, titled *Rooster Cogburn* (1975).

SPICY GRILLED CHICKEN BREASTS

Things are just hotter in the West, including this delicious chicken recipe.

SERVES 4

PROVISIONS

4   bone-in, skin-on chicken breasts
    Olive oil, for chicken
    Vegetable oil, for grill

SPICE RUB

2   Tbsp. brown sugar
1   Tbsp. smoked paprika
2   tsp. kosher or fine sea salt
1   tsp. garlic powder
1   tsp. onion powder
½   tsp. chipotle chili powder

SAUCE

2   Tbsp. butter
2   Tbsp. honey
1   Tbsp. hot sauce

DIRECTIONS

SPICE RUB

1. Combine all ingredients in a small bowl.

CHICKEN

1. Brush the chicken breasts with olive oil and rub liberally with the spice rub. Let sit for 15 minutes at room temperature.

2. Prepare grill for direct and indirect heat and preheat to medium-high.

3. Brush the grill grates with vegetable oil. Place the chicken breasts skin side up on the indirect heat side of the grill.

4. Grill with the lid closed for 15 minutes.

5. Flip the chicken and grill for 20 minutes or until an internal temperature of 160 degrees F is reached.

SAUCE

1. While chicken is grilling, heat the butter, honey and hot sauce together in a small saucepan.

2. When the chicken breasts have reached an internal temperature of 160 degrees F, brush with the sauce, move to the direct heat side of the grill and grill for 1 minute.

3. Brush with more sauce, flip and grill for another minute.

4. Remove chicken breasts from grill, brush with more sauce and serve.

Duke in another of his classic films.

WAYNE FAMILY TIP

For an added finishing touch of citrusy flavor, drizzle the juice of a lime over the chicken just before serving. You can also use lime wedges as a garnish when it comes time to plate the meal.

TIN STAR TURKEY BURGERS

These delicious burgers protect your stomach from the threat of hunger.

SERVES 4

PROVISIONS

- 2 cups fresh or frozen cranberries
- ⅔ cup sugar
- ⅔ cup orange juice
- 1½ lb. ground turkey
- Vegetable oil, for patties
- Kosher or fine sea salt, to taste
- Pepper, to taste
- 4 hamburger buns
- 2 Tbsp. melted butter

DIRECTIONS

1. Combine the cranberries, sugar and orange juice in a medium saucepan. Bring to a boil, stirring until the sugar dissolves. Lower the heat and simmer until most of the cranberries have burst, stirring occasionally. Remove from heat and let cool. The sauce will thicken as it cools.

2. Prepare the grill for direct heat and heat to medium-high.

3. Divide the turkey into 4 equal-sized portions. Form each portion into patties and make a depression in the center of each patty with your thumb. Brush the patties with oil and season with salt and pepper.

4. Grill the burgers for 4 minutes with the lid closed. Flip and cook another 4 minutes or until the burgers are cooked through.

5. Brush the hamburger buns with melted butter and grill lightly. Place a patty on the bottom half of the bun, top with cranberry sauce, the top bun and serve.

Rio Bravo,
1959

DID YOU KNOW?

When it came to hunting game, one of Duke's favorite grounds was near the White Mountains of Arizona. There, he would often stop at lodges for a game of cards with the locals.

CHOWTIME CHICKEN WINGS

You and yours will plow through these delicious wings in a matter of minutes!

SERVES 4 TO 6

PROVISIONS

MARINADE

- ¼ cup honey
- ½ tsp. ground ginger
- 1 garlic clove, minced
- 2 lb. chicken wings
- Vegetable oil, for grill

SAUCE

- ⅓ cup honey
- 1–2 Tbsp. Sriracha sauce (depending on how spicy you like it)
- 2 tsp. white sesame seeds

DIRECTIONS

1. Combine all the marinade ingredients in a mixing bowl and whisk well to combine.

2. Pour into a large food storage bag, add the chicken wings, squeeze out the excess air and seal.

3. Refrigerate for 2 to 12 hours, turning the bag occasionally.

4. Prepare grill for direct heat and preheat to medium-high.

5. Remove the chicken wings from the marinade, discarding the marinade.

6. Pat the wings dry with paper towels.

7. Brush the grill grates with oil.

8. Grill the wings 8 minutes per side or until the chicken is cooked through and the wings are darkly browned.

9. Combine the sauce ingredients in a small bowl and whisk well.

10. Brush the sauce on the wings and grill for 1 more minute per side.

11. Sprinkle with sesame seeds and serve.

The Sons of Katie Elder, 1965

New Frontier
Vegetable Salad,
Page 212

ON THE SIDE

★

EVEN DUKE NEEDED A SIDEKICK NOW AND THEN, AND YOU'LL BE GLAD TO HAVE THESE DISHES TO ROUND OUT YOUR MEALS.

ANGEL AND THE BADMAN BISCUITS

No matter how rough and tough your guests are,
they're sure to have a soft spot for these buttery biscuits.

MAKES ABOUT 16 BISCUITS

PROVISIONS

5½ tsp. dry active yeast

4 Tbsp. sugar, divided

¼ cup warm water

2 cups milk

2 Tbsp. apple cider vinegar

5 cups all-purpose flour, plus more for rolling out the dough

1½ tsp. baking powder

1 tsp. baking soda

1 tsp. kosher or fine sea salt

½ cup vegetable shortening

4 Tbsp. melted butter

DIRECTIONS

1. Combine yeast, 2 Tbsp. sugar and water in a small bowl. Whisk and let sit 5 minutes or until foamy.

2. Combine milk and apple cider vinegar and let sit for 5 minutes.

3. In a large bowl, whisk together the flour, baking powder, baking soda, 2 Tbsp. sugar and salt. Cut in the vegetable shortening until it resembles wet sand with some larger pieces of shortening. Add the yeast mixture and milk mixture. Stir to combine. Cover the bowl and let sit 1 hour. (Can also be stored in the refrigerator, covered, for up to 2 or 3 days— bring to room temperature before rolling out.)

4. Prepare the grill for indirect heat and preheat to high.

5. Flour a work surface and pat the dough out about 1½ inches thick. Cut out biscuits using a 2- to 3-in. round cookie cutter. Put biscuits in prepared skillets placing them close together. Brush the tops of the biscuits with more melted butter. Grill with the lid closed for 12 to 15 minutes or until the biscuits are golden brown, rotating the pan to keep the bottoms from burning.

6. Serve warm.

Angel and the Badman, 1947

J.B. BOOKS'S BLACK BEAN SALAD

This hearty side tastes so good, your family might just forget to tuck into the main course!

SERVES 6 TO 8

PROVISIONS

- 2 (15-oz.) cans black beans, drained and rinsed
- 1½ cups frozen (thawed) or fresh corn kernels
- 2 avocados, diced
- 1 large tomato, seeded and chopped
- ½ small red onion, diced
- 4 Tbsp. olive oil
- 2 Tbsp. lime juice
- 1 Tbsp. honey
- 2 tsp. hot sauce
- ¾ tsp. kosher or fine sea salt
- ¼ tsp. pepper
- ¼ tsp. ground cumin

DIRECTIONS

1. In a large bowl, combine the black beans, corn kernels, avocado, tomato and onion. In a small bowl, whisk together the olive oil, lime juice, honey, hot sauce, salt, pepper and cumin. Pour over the vegetables and toss well. Serve immediately or cover with plastic wrap and refrigerate for up to 4 hours.

DID YOU KNOW?

The Shootist opens with a montage of Duke's earlier films, which is meant to represent the life of gunslinger J.B. Books.

John Wayne in the 1976 film, *The Shootist*.

Kim Darby and
John Wayne in
True Grit, 1969.

CHEESY TRUE GRITS

This Southern staple is so undeniably delicious,
it might just earn you a long overdue award.

SERVES 6 TO 8

PROVISIONS

- 4 cups milk
- 1 cup stone ground grits
- 2 tsp. kosher or fine sea salt
- 4 oz. cream cheese
- 2 cups grated cheddar cheese
- 2 tsp. hot sauce
- 1 tsp. pepper
- 4 green onions, chopped

DIRECTIONS

1. Combine the milk, grits and salt
   in a saucepan and bring to a boil.
   Lower the heat and simmer until
   the grits are tender, about 20
   minutes. Stir in the cheeses, hot
   sauce and pepper. Cook until all
   the cheese has melted.

2. Transfer the grits to a serving
   bowl and top with the chopped
   green onions.

WAYNE FAMILY TIP

If you want your grits a little
saltier, do all the salting before
the grits are cooked. Cooked
grits won't absorb salt, so salt the
water or the dry grits before you
get too far into cooking.

John Wayne and Ella Raines (right) flank Frank Puglia in a scene from *Tall in the Saddle* (1944). The movie's screenplay was co-written by Paul Fix, who usually worked in front of the camera as a supporting actor in many Westerns.

McLINTOCK COLESLAW

Once you serve up this essential side, everyone will be begging you to give up the recipe.

SERVES 6

PROVISIONS

½ cup sour cream

½ cup mayonnaise

2 tsp. sugar

2 limes, juiced

1 (14- to 16-oz.) bag coleslaw mix

4 green onions, thinly sliced

½ cup fresh cilantro, chopped

    Kosher salt and freshly ground black pepper, to taste

DIRECTIONS

1. In a large mixing bowl, combine the sour cream, mayonnaise, sugar and lime juice, whisking until smooth. Add the coleslaw, green onions and cilantro. Toss to combine. Season to taste with salt and pepper.

John Wayne in *McLintock!*, 1963.

DID YOU KNOW?

John Wayne shared the screen with his friend, actress Maureen O'Hara, on five occasions, including the critically revered 1963 comedic Western, *McLintock!*

WAYNE FAMILY TIP

If you buy potatoes ahead of time, never store them in the refrigerator. Potatoes keep their texture best in a place that's dark and cool, not cold.

3 GODFATHERS GARLIC POTATOES

It would be a crime not to serve these delicious spuds at your next get-together.

SERVES 6

PROVISIONS

- **2** lb. baby Yukon Gold potatoes (¾-inch diameter), washed and unpeeled
- **1** large white onion, cut in half widthwise and each half cut into 6 wedges
- **4** Tbsp. unsalted butter, cut into small pieces
- **3** garlic cloves, chopped
- **1** tsp. garlic powder
- **2** tsp. kosher or fine sea salt
- **1** tsp. freshly ground black pepper

DIRECTIONS

1. Prepare the grill for direct heat and preheat to medium.

2. Place the potatoes in a cast-iron skillet in a single layer. Add the rest of the ingredients, stir well and cover the skillet snugly with foil. Put the pan over indirect heat and cover the grill. Cook for 30 minutes, remove foil, stir and cook uncovered for another 10 minutes or until the potatoes are tender.

3. To keep warm until serving, cover the pan with foil. The residual heat from the pan will keep the potatoes warm.

3 Godfathers,
1948

GREEN BERET
GREEN BEANS AND BACON

Your family will be standing at attention once they get a bite of this hearty side.

SERVES 4 TO 6

PROVISIONS

- 1   lb. green beans, trimmed
- 3   Tbsp. olive oil
- 1   Tbsp. red wine vinegar
- 1½ tsp. Dijon mustard
- 4   slices bacon, cooked and crumbled
- ½   pint cherry tomatoes, halved
-     Kosher or fine sea salt, to taste
-     Pepper, to taste

DIRECTIONS

1. Bring a large pot of salted water to a boil. Prepare a large bowl filled with ice water. Drop the beans into the boiling water and cook until crisp tender, about 4 minutes. Remove the beans from the boiling water and place directly in the ice water. Let cool at least 5 minutes. Drain well.

2. In a salad bowl, whisk together the oil, vinegar and mustard. Add the drained beans, bacon and tomatoes. Toss to coat. Add salt and pepper to taste.

Duke with sons Patrick and Michael on set of *The Green Berets* (1968).

DID YOU KNOW?

Duke's character in *The Green Berets*, Col. Mike Kirby, is based on a real World War II Finnish army captain named Lauri Törni, who later went by the name Larry Thorne.

WAYNE ✕ **FAMILY**
TIP

When preparing this salad, you can really brighten the flavor by adding a simple squeeze of lime juice just before serving. Plus, the juice will keep some of the necessary moisture intact.

BUCKAROO BREAD SALAD

You may not think "bread" or "salad" when you think "barbecue," but this dish will make you think again, pilgrim.

SERVES 6 TO 8

PROVISIONS

- 1   baguette
- ½   cup olive oil, plus more for brushing the bread and peppers
- 1   tsp. kosher or fine sea salt, plus more to taste
- 2   yellow bell peppers
- 1   pint cherry tomatoes, halved
- 1   seedless cucumber, chopped
- ½   small red onion, thinly sliced
- 20 basil leaves
- 3   Tbsp. white wine vinegar
- 1   garlic clove, minced
- ½   tsp. pepper

DIRECTIONS

1. Prepare the grill for direct heat and preheat to medium-high.

2. Cut the baguette in half, brush with olive oil and sprinkle with salt. Cut the peppers in half, pull out the seeds and veins and brush with olive oil.

3. Grill the bread until it is charred, 2 to 3 minutes. Grill the peppers, cut side down, until they are charred and begin to soften, about 4 minutes.

4. Cut the bread into bite-sized pieces and place in a salad bowl. Chop the peppers and add to the bread. Add the tomatoes, cucumber and onion. Stack the basil leaves on a cutting board, roll up like a cigar and thinly slice. Add to the bread and vegetables.

5. In a small bowl, whisk together ½ cup olive oil, vinegar, garlic, salt and pepper. Pour over the salad and toss. Serve or allow to sit at room temperature for 30 minutes to let the flavors meld.

Ride Him Cowboy, 1932

CAVALRY CORN

Your friends will gallop to the dinner table once they catch a whiff of these cooking on the grill.

SERVES 6

PROVISIONS

- 6 ears of corn, unhusked
- 1 tsp. kosher or fine sea salt, plus more to taste
- ½ cup butter, at room temperature
- 1 lime
- 2 tsp. chili powder
- Pepper, to taste

DIRECTIONS

1. Pull the outer husks of the corn ears down to the base. Pull out the corn silk from each and fold the husks back in place.

2. Fill a large pot or bowl with cold water and add 1 Tbsp. of salt. Let the corn soak for at least 30 minutes or up to 4 hours.

3. Prepare the grill for direct and indirect heat and preheat to medium. Remove the corn from the water shaking off the excess. Place the corn on the direct heat side of the grill and cook with the lid closed for 4 to 5 minutes or until nicely charred. Move the corn to the indirect heat side and cook with the lid closed for another 10 to 15 minutes or until the corn kernels are tender when pierced with a paring knife.

4. Put the butter in a small bowl. Grate the lime zest into the butter and squeeze in the juice. Add the chili powder and a large pinch of salt and pepper and stir well.

5. Serve the corn hot with the butter.

Duke in action in *Rio Grande*, 1950.

DID YOU KNOW?

The 1950 cavalry Western *Rio Grande* marked the on-screen debut of Patrick Wayne. John Wayne's sons Michael, Patrick and Ethan would sometimes appear in his films.

Duke rides tall in the saddle in a scene from one of his films.

DID YOU KNOW?

Duke's favorite horse, Dollor, appears in six of the legend's films. While filming *The Shootist*, John Wayne even had the script changed so that he could call Dollor by name.

BUCKING BRONCO BAKED BEANS

Hold onto your hat—these beans come with quite a kick!

SERVES 10 TO 12

PROVISIONS

2   Tbsp. olive oil

1   lb. bacon, chopped

1   medium white or yellow onion, diced

2   garlic cloves, minced

1   jalapeño pepper, seeded, deveined and minced

3   (15-oz.) cans pork and beans

½   cup brewed coffee

¼   cup ketchup

¼   cup brown sugar

2   Tbsp. chili powder

1   Tbsp. Worcestershire sauce

1   tsp. dry mustard

    Kosher or fine sea salt, to taste

    Pepper, to taste

DIRECTIONS

1. Preheat oven to 325 degrees F.

2. Heat oil in a large Dutch oven over medium-high. Add the bacon and cook until it starts to brown and renders its fat, about 5 minutes. Add the onion and cook until softened, about 5 minutes. Add the garlic and jalapeño pepper and cook for 1 minute. Add the rest of the ingredients, stir well and cook uncovered for 1 hour 15 minutes.

Duke enjoys some time with wife Pilar, daughter Marisa and son Ethan at their home in Newport Beach, California. The Waynes moved to Newport in the mid-1960s.

MA'S OLD-TIMEY BAKED POTATOES

These potatoes pack a robust flavor worthy of the John Wayne name.

SERVES 4

PROVISIONS

- 4 medium russet baking potatoes, washed
- ½ cup melted butter
- 2 Tbsp. chopped fresh chives
- 1 tsp. garlic powder
- 1 tsp. kosher or fine sea salt (if using salted butter, use only ½ tsp.)
- ½ tsp. pepper

DIRECTIONS

1. Prepare the grill for indirect heat and preheat to medium-high.

2. Cut 12 slices into each potato, cutting almost to the bottom—do not cut all the way through. Place the potatoes in the microwave and cook on high power for 10 minutes. (If your microwave does not have a turntable, rotate the potatoes after 5 minutes.)

3. Combine the melted butter with the chives, garlic powder, salt and pepper.

4. Lay four 14- by 12-in. pieces of foil on a work surface. Place a potato in the center of each piece and brush with the chive butter. Bring the side of foil up and fold over making sure to seal well. Place the potatoes on the indirect heat side of the grill and cook with the lid closed for 30 to 40 minutes or until the potatoes are tender.

5. Carefully unwrap the potatoes and serve.

Duke with his mother, Mary "Molly" Brown.

SWEET PEACH SALAD

Serve this salad when the sun's beating down and everyone's hunger is heating up.

SERVES 4 TO 6

PROVISIONS

- 3 ripe peaches
-    Vegetable oil, for brushing
- 5 oz. washed baby spinach
- 4 green onions, sliced
- 2 tsp. sugar
- 3 slices thick cut bacon
- 1 Tbsp. red wine vinegar

DIRECTIONS

1. Prepare the grill for direct heat and preheat to medium-high.

2. Cut the peaches in half and cut each half into 3 wedges. Brush the cut sides with oil. Grill 2 to 3 minutes per cut side or until nice grill marks are achieved but the peaches are still a little firm. Remove from grill and let cool.

3. Place the spinach in a salad bowl with the green onions and sprinkle the sugar all over.

4. Place the bacon in a cold skillet, turn the heat to medium and cook until very crisp, about 8 minutes, turning occasionally. Drain on paper towels and crumble. Add the vinegar to the skillet carefully (it will splatter) and cook until thickened, about 30 seconds. Pour the hot salad dressing over the spinach and toss to coat. Top with the grilled peaches and crumbled bacon. Serve immediately.

Duke in Monument Valley.

WAYNE **FAMILY**

TIP

When shopping for peaches, you can test for ripeness by noticing a peach's color and firmness. Look for peaches that are dark yellow and have a little give when you grip them.

NEW FRONTIER VEGETABLE SALAD

This simple, satisfying salad can take your barbecue to new territories.

PROVISIONS

3 red or yellow peppers, or a combination

¾ cup olive oil

⅓ cup balsamic vinegar

2 tsp. dried oregano

1 tsp. kosher or fine sea salt

½ tsp. pepper

1 large or 2 small eggplants

1 large white onion, cut into ½-in. slices

4 cups arugula

4 slices bacon, cooked and crumbled

DIRECTIONS

1. Prepare grill for direct heat and preheat to medium-high.

2. Place the peppers on the grill whole and grill with the lid closed until the skin is blackened all over, turning occasionally, about 6 minutes. Remove from the grill, place in a bowl and cover with plastic wrap. Let cool at room temperature.

3. Whisk together the olive oil, vinegar, oregano, salt and pepper.

4. Slice the eggplant into ¼-in. thick slices and brush both sides with the oil and vinegar mixture. Brush the onion slices with the oil and vinegar mixture. Grill with the lid close until slightly charred and beginning to soften, about 4 to 5 minutes per side. Remove from the grill and brush again with the oil and vinegar mixture. Let cool.

5. When the peppers are cool enough to handle, scrape off the skins, cut in half and pull out the seeds and veins. Cut into ¼-in. thick strips and brush with the oil and vinegar mixture.

6. Toss the arugula with 3 Tbsp. of the oil and vinegar mixture. Place the arugula on a platter, top with the grilled vegetables and scatter the bacon over the top.

A young John Wayne in *The New Frontier*, 1935.

STAR PACKER POTATO SALAD

You'll never need to face off against a hungry crowd with this recipe up your sleeve.

SERVES 6 TO 8

PROVISIONS

- 3 lb. Yukon gold potatoes, peeled and cut into 1 in. pieces
- 2 Tbsp. plus 1 tsp. kosher or fine sea salt, divided
- 2 Tbsp. olive oil
- 1 Tbsp. white wine vinegar
- ½ tsp. pepper
- ⅓ cup mayonnaise
- ⅓ cup sour cream
- 6 green onions, thinly sliced
- 3 celery ribs, diced
- 1 Tbsp. minced chives

DIRECTIONS

1. Place the potatoes in a large pan and fill with cold water. Add 2 Tbsp. salt and bring to a boil. Reduce heat and simmer until the potatoes are tender, about 15 minutes. Drain and return the potatoes to the hot pot. Add the olive oil, vinegar, 1 tsp. salt, pepper and stir to coat the potatoes well. Let sit at room temperature to cool. Once the potatoes have cooled, transfer to a large mixing bowl. Add the mayonnaise, sour cream, green onions, celery and chives. Stir well. Taste and add more salt and pepper if needed. Cover and refrigerate until cold, at least 4 hours. Can be made 1 to 2 days ahead.

John Wayne in the 1934 film *The Star Packer*.

DID YOU KNOW?

The Matlock ranch-house that appears in John Wayne's 1934 film *The Star Packer* is also used in two other Duke-starring films, 1934's *Blue Steel* and 1935's *The Desert Trail*.

John Wayne and Kirk Douglas chow down in a scene from *The War Wagon* (1967). Douglas, who proves a deft hand with the chopsticks, also worked with Duke in *In Harm's Way* (1965) and *Cast a Giant Shadow* (1966).

TEX-MEX MAC AND CHEESE

Everything's bigger in Texas, so save room on the side for this plentiful dish.

SERVES 8 TO 10

PROVISIONS

Kosher or fine sea salt, to taste

1   lb. macaroni

¼   cup butter

¼   cup flour

2½ cups whole milk

¾   lb. cheddar cheese, grated

½   lb. Monterey Jack cheese, grated

2   (10-oz.) cans tomatoes and chilies, drained

¾   tsp. pepper

1   Tbsp. hot sauce, optional

4   cups tortilla chips

DIRECTIONS

1. Preheat oven to 350 degrees F. Grease a 9- by 12-in. deep-dish baking pan.

2. Bring a large pot of salted water to a boil. Add the macaroni and cook according to the package directions. Drain.

3. In a large skillet, melt the butter over medium heat. Whisk in the flour and cook, whisking, for 1 minute. Add the milk and cook, whisking often, until thickened, about 5 minutes. Reserve about 1 cup cheddar cheese and add the rest to the sauce along with the Monterey Jack cheese, canned tomatoes and chilies, pepper and hot sauce. Cook until all the cheese has melted. Add the drained macaroni and stir well. Pour the mixture into the prepared baking dish and top with the reserved cheddar cheese.

4. Place the tortilla chips in a large food storage bag, seal and crush the chips with a rolling pin. Spread the crushed tortilla chips over the top of the cheese.

5. Bake for 25 to 30 minutes and serve.

Duke directing *The Alamo*, 1960.

ALL-AMERICAN WATERMELON SALAD

Even if you can take all the heat of an Arizona sun,
it never hurts to cool off with a summer salad like this one.

SERVES 6 TO 8

PROVISIONS

- 1   (5-lb.) seedless watermelon, flesh cut into 1-in. cubes
- 1   large (approximately 1 lb.) sweet onion, diced
- ½   cup olive oil
- ¼   cup balsamic vinegar
- ¼   cup chopped fresh mint leaves, plus mint sprigs for garnish
- 1   tsp. kosher salt
- ½   tsp. freshly ground black pepper
- 4   oz. crumbled feta cheese

DIRECTIONS

1. Combine the watermelon and onion in a mixing bowl. Whisk together the oil, vinegar, chopped mint, salt and pepper. Pour over the watermelon and onion and toss to coat. Add the crumbled feta and toss gently. Serve garnished with fresh mint sprigs if desired.

2. This salad is best served immediately, but it can be made ahead and chilled in the refrigerator. If the salad develops a lot of liquid after chilling, transfer to a serving dish with a slotted spoon.

Duke with his children Ethan and Marisa.

No-Bake
Banana Split Pie,
Page 243

DUKE'S
DESSERTS

★

TOPPING OFF A BBQ FEAST
WITH A SWEET DISH IS AS
AMERICAN AS APPLE PIE.

WAYNE FAMILY TIP

Before you even begin preparing to make these cookies, set out your butter and eggs so they reach room temperature. At room temperature, they mix better with the dry ingredients.

CHOCOLATE CHIP COOKIE ICE CREAM SANDWICHES

Like the dynamic duo of John Wayne and John Ford, this dessert is a winning combination of flavors.

MAKES 8 SANDWICHES

PROVISIONS

½ cup butter, melted and cooled

½ cup sugar

⅓ cup brown sugar, packed

2 tsp. vanilla extract

1 large egg

1 cup flour

½ tsp. kosher or fine sea salt

¼ tsp. baking soda

½ cup mini chocolate chips

2 pints vanilla ice cream

DIRECTIONS

1. Preheat oven to 375 degrees F. Line 2 baking sheets with parchment paper or silicone baking mats.

2. In a mixer beat the butter and sugars together on medium-high speed until creamy. Turn the mixer to low and beat in the vanilla and egg. Add the flour, salt and baking soda and beat on low until the mixture forms into dough. Stir in the chocolate chips.

3. Roll the dough into 16 large balls. Place on baking sheets and flatten slightly with the back of a spatula. Bake for 9 to 12 minutes or until golden. Let cool on pan for 5 minutes then remove to a wire rack to finish cooling completely.

4. Place a scoop of ice cream on the flat side of half the cookies. Top with another cookie, flat side down and gently press together. Place in the freezer for at least 1 hour before serving.

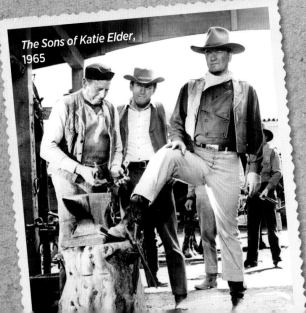

The Sons of Katie Elder, 1965

GRILLED COWBOY COBBLER

Just because you're the toughest son-of-a-gun around doesn't mean you can't enjoy this dessert.

SERVES 6

PROVISIONS

1½ cups biscuit mix (Bisquick)

½ cup plus 2 Tbsp. sugar, divided

1 cup milk

4 Tbsp. butter

1½ cups fresh or frozen (thawed) peach slices

1 cup fresh or frozen (thawed) blueberries

DIRECTIONS

1. Prepare grill for direct and indirect heat and preheat to medium.

2. Combine the biscuit mix, ½ cup sugar and milk. Mix until smooth.

3. Put the butter in an 8-inch disposable foil cake pan and place on the grill over direct heat until the butter is melted. Swirl the butter to coat the pan. Pour the batter over the butter and top with the peach slices and blueberries. Sprinkle with 2 Tbsp. sugar.

4. Place the pan back on the grill over indirect heat, close the lid and cook for 30 minutes or until the edges are golden brown and a toothpick inserted into the center comes out clean. Can be served warm, at room temperature or cold.

Duke plays a game of chess, 1972.

DID YOU KNOW?

When he wasn't busy making movies, Duke enjoyed spending his down time playing games of chess. The legend even had a permanent chess board installed on his yacht, the *Wild Goose*.

John Wayne in
The Comancheros (1961).

DID YOU KNOW?

Although most of *The Comancheros* was directed by Michael Curtiz, Duke had to step into the role of director for some scenes when his friend Curtiz fell ill.

HOMESTEAD APPLE CRISP

Like a John Wayne film, this dessert is a classic you'll keep coming back to time and again.

SERVES 6 TO 8

PROVISIONS

APPLES

- 8 medium apples, peeled, cored, and sliced
- 1 lemon, juiced
- ¼ cup brown sugar, packed
- 1 tsp. ground cinnamon
- 1 tsp. vanilla extract
- ⅛ tsp. kosher or fine sea salt
- 3 Tbsp. butter

TOPPING

- 1 cup oats
- 1 cup brown sugar, packed
- ¼ cup flour
- 1 Tbsp. ground cinnamon
- ½ tsp. kosher or fine sea salt
- ¼ tsp. ground nutmeg
- ¼ cup cold butter, cut into small pieces

DIRECTIONS

1. Prepare grill for indirect heat and preheat to medium.

APPLES

1. In a large bowl, combine all the ingredients for the apples, except the butter. Let sit for 5 minutes.

TOPPING

1. In another bowl, combine the oats, brown sugar, flour, cinnamon, salt and nutmeg. Add the butter and work in with your fingers until evenly mixed.

2. Melt the 3 Tbsp. butter in a 9-inch cast iron skillet. Add the apples and toss with the butter. Sprinkle the topping evenly on top of the apples. Grill over indirect heat with the lid closed for 30 to 35 minutes, turning the pan occasionally.

Duke in a scene from *The Big Trail* (1930). The movie was the first time Marion Morrison was credited as John Wayne.

McQ'S MOLASSES COOKIES

John Wayne loved these classic cookies, and it's easy to see why—
their taste is as timeless as the man himself.

MAKES 2 ½ TO 3 DOZEN COOKIES

PROVISIONS

2¼ cups flour

2½ tsp. baking soda

1   tsp. ground cinnamon

1   tsp. dried ginger

½   tsp. ground cloves

½   tsp. kosher or fine sea salt

½   cup vegetable shortening, at room temperature

¼   cup butter, at room temperature

½   cup brown sugar, packed

1   large egg

¼   cup molasses

2   tsp. vanilla extract

½   cup sugar

DIRECTIONS

1. Preheat oven to 350 degrees F. Line 2 baking sheets with parchment paper or silicone baking mats. In a large bowl, whisk together the flour, baking soda, cinnamon, ginger, cloves and salt.

2. In a mixer, combine the shortening, butter, brown sugar, egg, molasses and vanilla. Beat until fully combined. Add the flour mixture and beat just until the mixture forms into a dough. Using a spatula, give the dough a final mix by hand.

3. Pour the sugar into a small bowl. Shape tablespoonfuls of dough into balls and roll in the sugar. Place on the baking sheets 2 inches apart.

4. Bake 10 to 12 minutes.

John Wayne takes aim in *McQ*, 1974.

DID YOU KNOW?

As a testament to his vitality and unmatched work ethic, John Wayne was 66 years old when he stepped into the role of the titular cop in the 1974 John Sturges-directed film, *McQ*.

SHERIFF'S FRUIT SKEWERS

Reach for these refreshing skewers when you need to satisfy that sweet tooth.

MAKES 20 TO 25 SKEWERS

PROVISIONS

20–25 wooden skewers

¾ cup balsamic vinegar

3 Tbsp. sugar

1 small seedless watermelon

1 honeydew melon

2 pints strawberries, hulled

Vegetable oil, for grill

DIRECTIONS

1. Soak the skewers in water for 30 minutes.

2. Prepare the grill for direct heat and preheat to medium-high.

3. In a small saucepan, combine the vinegar and sugar. Bring to a boil over high heat stirring just until the sugar dissolves. Continue to boil the mixture for 5 to 6 minutes or until the consistency of syrup. The mixture will thicken as it cools. Let cool.

4. Cut out the flesh of the watermelon and cut into 1-inch cubes. Cut out of the flesh of the honey dew melon and cut into 1-inch pieces.

5. Thread the melon pieces and strawberries onto the skewers. Brush the grill grates with oil. Grill skewers for about 2 minutes per side (for a total of 8 minutes) with the lid open.

6. Serve the skewers with the balsamic glaze.

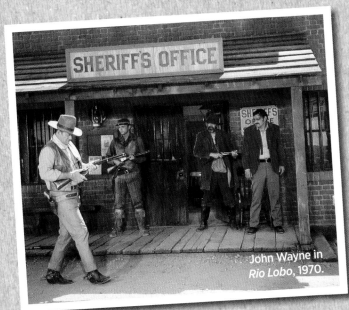

John Wayne in *Rio Lobo*, 1970.

DID YOU KNOW?

When John Wayne's character Col. Cord McNally visits the sherrif's office in *Rio Lobo*, there is a wanted poster for Hondo Lane, Duke's character in the film *Hondo*.

GEORGIA PEACH MELBAS

You can't go wrong with this crowd-pleasing dessert that will have 'em asking for thirds.

SERVES 6

PROVISIONS

RASPBERRY SAUCE

- 1 (12-oz.) bag frozen raspberries, thawed
- 2 Tbsp. sugar
- 1 Tbsp. lemon juice

PEACHES

- 3 large peaches, firm but ripe
- 3 Tbsp. melted butter
- 3 Tbsp. sugar
- Vegetable oil, for grill
- 1½ pints vanilla ice cream
- 6 mint sprigs

DIRECTIONS

SAUCE

1. Combine the raspberries, sugar and lemon juice in a blender and puree. Strain through a fine mesh strainer. Can be made 2 days ahead. Store covered in the refrigerator until ready to serve.

PEACHES

1. Prepare the grill for direct heat and preheat to medium high.

2. Cut the peaches in half and remove the pits. Combine the butter and sugar in a small bowl. Brush the sugar mixture thickly on the cut sides of the peaches.

3. Brush the grill grates with oil. Grill the peaches, cut side down 5 to 6 minutes or until nicely marked and just starting to soften.

4. Place a little raspberry sauce on the bottom of each serving plate, top with a peach half, a scoop of ice cream, more raspberry sauce and a mint sprig. Serve immediately.

Duke takes a slugger's stance.

DID YOU KNOW?

While John Wayne was a bonafide tough guy on the screen, he had a major sweet tooth. His daughter Marisa recalls trips on the town often ended with ice cream.

WAYNE FAMILY TIP

Pineapple slices can be a little tricky to handle on the grill. For easier handling, you can cut the slices into wedges and then gently thread them onto skewers before grilling.

HAWAIIAN PINEAPPLE AND ICE CREAM

Duke spent much of his personal and professional life in Hawaii, and a serving of this sweet will make you feel like you're on the Big Island, too.

SERVES 6

PROVISIONS

- ½ cup sweetened coconut flakes
- 1 whole pineapple
- ½ cup cream of coconut
- Vegetable oil, for grill
- 1½ pints dulce de leche ice cream
- 6 mint sprigs

DIRECTIONS

1. Put the coconut in a dry skillet and cook over medium heat, stirring until toasted, about 3 to 4 minutes. Let cool.

2. Prepare grill for direct heat and preheat to medium-high.

3. Cut the top and bottom off the pineapple, then cut off the skin. Slice the pineapple into 6 slices about ½-in. thick. Brush both side of the pineapple with the cream of coconut and let sit for 5 to 10 minutes while the grill pre-heats. Brush the grill grates with oil and grill the pineapple 4 to 5 minutes per side with the lid closed. Let cool.

4. Serve the pineapple slices with a scoop of ice cream and top with the toasted coconut. Garnish with mint sprigs.

John Wayne, wife Pilar and daughter Aissa.

FIGHTING SEABEE BANANA BOATS

Break out this dish when you need some heavy artillery to fend off intense cravings.

SERVES 4

PROVISIONS

- 4 medium unpeeled bananas
- 4 Tbsp. semisweet chocolate chips
- 4 Tbsp. caramel bits
- 4 Tbsp. mini marshmallows
- 4 graham crackers

DIRECTIONS

1. Prepare the grill for direct heat.

2. With a sharp knife, make a deep cut lengthwise along the inside curve of the banana being careful not to cut all the way through. Open the slit to form a pocket. Fill each banana with 1 Tbsp. each of chocolate chips, toffee bits and mini marshmallows. Crumble a graham cracker on top of each. Wrap each banana with a piece of foil making sure to seal the edges well.

3. Grill covered for 10 minutes. Unwrap the bananas and serve.

WAYNE FAMILY TIP

These banana boats are perfect for family camping trips when everyone is sitting around the fire. If you have extra nuts on hand, like pecans or walnuts, try adding a handful for extra crunch.

John Wayne in *The Fighting Seabees*, 1944.

NO-BAKE BANANA SPLIT PIE

There's no need for two desserts to duel when they can come together as one unbeatable dish

SERVES 8

PROVISIONS

2 cups graham cracker crumbs

½ cup melted butter

4 oz. cream cheese, at room temperature

3 cups heavy whipping cream

⅓ cup powdered sugar

3 large bananas, sliced

1 pint strawberries, hulled and sliced

1 (20-oz.) can crushed pineapple, drained well

½ cup chopped walnuts

Chocolate syrup

8–10 maraschino cherries, patted dry

DIRECTIONS

1. Combine the graham cracker crumbs with the melted butter and press firmly into a 9-in. deep dish pie pan. Refrigerate while preparing the filling.

2. Beat the cream cheese with a mixer until smooth. In a clean mixing bowl whip the cream with the powdered sugar until stiff peaks form.

3. Combine one third of the whipped cream with the cream cheese, mixing well. Spread onto the crust. Top with sliced bananas, strawberries and pineapple, in that order. Spread the remaining whipped cream on top of the pie. Refrigerate for 4 hours or up to a day ahead.

4. Before serving, sprinkle the walnuts on top of the pie, drizzle with chocolate syrup and place maraschino cherries on top.

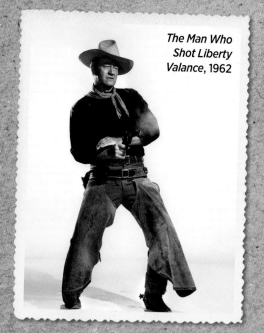

The Man Who Shot Liberty Valance, 1962

DID YOU KNOW?

The Man Who Shot Liberty Valance was Duke's last black-and-white film. While technicolor was available, director John Ford claimed black-and-white added to the tension in the film.

Duke in a scene from *Rio Bravo* (1959).

CONVERSION GUIDE

Use this handy chart to convert cups and ounces to liters and grams.

VOLUME

¼ teaspoon	=	1 mL
½ teaspoon	=	2 mL
1 teaspoon	=	5 mL
1 tablespoon	=	15 mL
¼ cup	=	50 mL
⅓ cup	=	75 mL
½ cup	=	125 mL
⅔ cup	=	150 mL
¾ cup	=	175 mL
1 cup	=	250 mL
1 quart	=	1 liter
1½ quarts	=	1.5 liters
2 quarts	=	2 liters
2½ quarts	=	2.5 liters
3 quarts	=	3 liters
4 quarts	=	4 liters

WEIGHT

1 ounce	=	30 grams
2 ounces	=	55 grams
3 ounces	=	85 grams
4 ounces (¼ pound)	=	115 grams
8 ounces (½ pound)	=	225 grams
16 ounces (1 pound)	=	445 grams
1 pound	=	455 grams
2 pounds	=	910 grams

LENGTH

⅛ inch	=	3 mm
¼ inch	=	6 mm
½ inch	=	13 mm
¾ inch	=	19 mm
1 inch	=	2.5 cm
2 inches	=	5 cm

TEMPERATURES

Fahrenheit		Celsius
32°	=	0°
212°	=	100°
250°	=	120°
275°	=	140°
300°	=	150°
325°	=	160°
350°	=	180°
375°	=	190°
400°	=	200°
425°	=	220°
450°	=	230°
475°	=	240°
500°	=	260°

INDEX

Molasses, 71, 101, 116, 232
Mushrooms, 46
Mustard
    Dijon, 21, 87, 102, 161, 198
    spicy brown, 45, 109

N

Nuts
    pine, 27
    walnuts, 243

O

Oats, 229
Olives, Kalamata, 88
Onions, 32, 41, 49, 138
    green, 60, 78, 106, 191,
        194, 210, 215
    French-fried, canned, 65
    red, 13, 28, 46, 71, 81, 84,
        88, 115, 147, 158, 168,
        188, 201
    sweet, 221
    white, 18, 28, 45, 60, 98,
        101, 106, 122, 141, 142,
        157, 197, 205, 212
    yellow, 18, 98, 106, 157, 205
Orange(s), 168
    juice, *see Juice*
    marmalade, 77, 87, 168

P

Peaches, 210, 226, 236

Peppers
    chipotle, in adobo sauce, 84
    green bell, 32, 46, 98, 122,
        142, 162
    jalapeño, 27, 28, 32, 60, 78,
        106, 115, 148, 157,
        158, 205
    orange bell, 32
    red bell, 32, 46, 60, 95, 98,
        122, 133, 142, 162, 212
    yellow bell, 32, 162, 201, 212
Pineapple
    chunks, canned, 95
    crushed, canned, 243
    juice, *see Juice*
    whole, 239
Pork
    and beans, 205
    baby back ribs, 101, 105
    burgers, *see Burgers*
    butt roast, 119
    ground, 41, 84, 92
    ham steak, 91
    loin chops, 78, 102
    loin roast, 109
    pulled, 115, 116
    prosciutto, 112
    tenderloins, 77, 81, 87, 88,
        95, 106, 112, 125
Potatoes
    russett baking, 209
    Yukon gold, 106, 197, 215

R

Radicchio, 13
Raspberries, frozen, 236

S

Salad
    All-American
        Watermelon, 221
    Buckaroo Bread, 201
    Gunslinger Steak, 13
    Grilled Chicken Caesar, 161
    Grilled Pork Tenderloin, 88
    J.B. Book's Black Bean, 188
    New Frontier Vegetable, 212
    Star Packer Potato, 215
    Sweet Peach, 210
Salsa, 32, 72, 133, 142, 162
Sandwiches
    Backcountry Sausage, 98
    Barbecue Beef, 71
    BLT Steak, 35
    Chocolate Chip Cookie
        Ice Cream, 225
    Pony Express Pulled Pork, 116
Sauce
    barbecue, 13, 41, 65, 77, 147
    hot, 101, 135, 167, 178, 188,
        191, 218
    soy, 21, 36, 95, 167
    Sriracha, 18, 77, 170, 182
    Tabasco, 71
    Worcestershire, 21, 35, 45,
        59, 71, 77, 119, 128, 135,
        145, 205
Sausages
    breakfast, 122
    Italian, 98, 122
Sesame seeds, 182
Shallots, 66

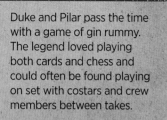

Duke and Pilar pass the time with a game of gin rummy. The legend loved playing both cards and chess and could often be found playing on set with costars and crew members between takes.

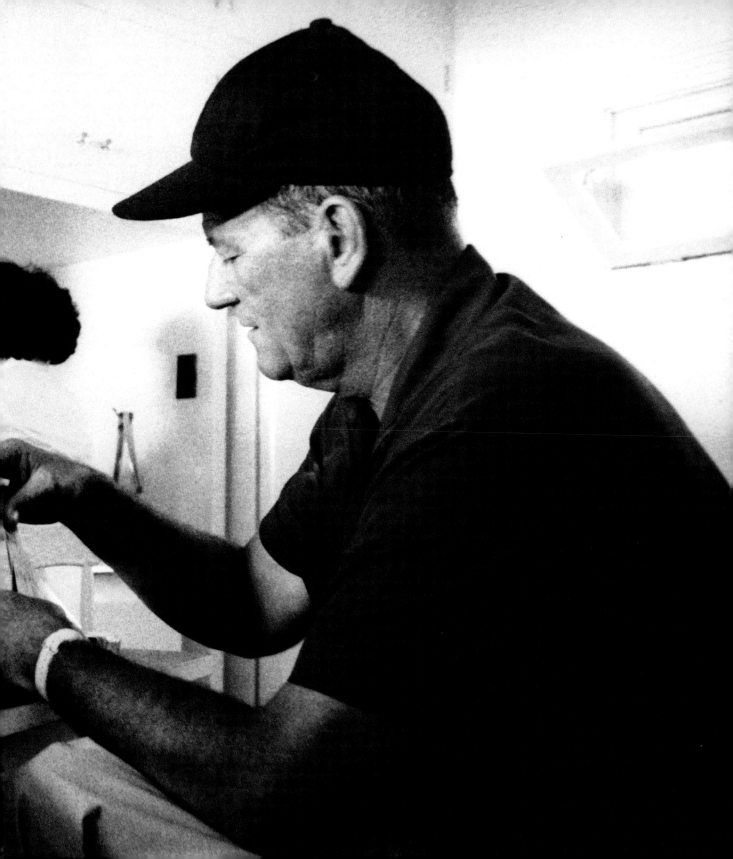

Media Lab Books
For inquiries, call 646-838-6637

Copyright 2017 Topix Media Lab

Published by Topix Media Lab
14 Wall Street, Suite 4B
New York, NY 10005

Printed in China

ISBN-10: 1-942556-50-0
ISBN-13: 978-1-942556-50-3

CEO Tony Romando

Vice President of Brand Marketing Joy Bomba
Director of Finance Vandana Patel
Director of Sales and New Markets Tom Mifsud
Manufacturing Director Nancy Puskuldjian
Financial Analyst Matthew Quinn
Brand Marketing Assistant Taylor Hamilton

Editor-in-Chief Jeff Ashworth
Creative Director Steven Charny
Photo Director Dave Weiss
Managing Editor Courtney Kerrigan
Senior Editor Tim Baker

Content Editor James Ellis
Content Designer Michelle Lock
Art Director Susan Dazzo
Assistant Managing Editor Holland Baker
Designer Danielle Santucci
Assistant Photo Editor Catherine Armanasco
Assistant Editors Trevor Courneen, Alicia Kort, Kaytie Norman

Co-Founders Bob Lee, Tony Romando

JOHN WAYNE
ENTERPRISES